WHERE TH

TROD

A story of Sussex shoemakers

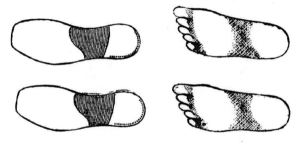

Wood engraving by Albion Russell c 1840

José Loosemore

CGB Books

J. Loosemore
Cordwainer's
The Street
Chiddingly, Lewes
East Sussex BN8 6HE
Tel. no. 01825-872637

For
MICHAEL AND MOLLY BROMLEY
who have had faith in me – someone who turned up out
of the blue and claimed kinship – and from whom
I have received great kindness and affection.

First published in Great Britain
in 1998 by CGB Books 53 South Street, Lewes, East Sussex BN7 2BU
in association with the author

©1998 José Loosemoore

ISBN 1 873983 01 8

Designed and typeset by CGB, Lewes
Printed by Island Press
3 Cradle Hill Industrial Estate, Seaford, East Sussex BN25 3JE
Tel: 01323 490222

CONTENTS

ACKNOWLEDGEMENTS

THERE are many people to thank for the way things have turned out, not least Michael and Molly Bromley. I needed a retreat from dear Chiddingly, which like my great great grandfather before me, claims so much of my time in village affairs – and the Bromleys put their lovely holiday home in Cornwall at my disposal. There, with my second husband Edward Loosemore, who kept the domestic chores at bay, I was able to concentrate on this saga.

Had it not been for Tess and David Llewellyn I might have abandoned the project in the early stages. They introduced me to their computer and processed my hand written pages and gave them a semblance of order from which it was so much easier to work. Julia Hunt came to the rescue when more typing was needed and the final draft was put onto disk for me by Angela Rose.

I am indebted to my cousin, Joy Holdsworth, for much family information; to Uckfield historian Norman Edwards for details about George Clifford Russell's businesses in that town; and to Steve Benz of S. B. Publications for his helpful advice on producing this book.

This is a reprint of a book which was first published in 1998. I have, since that time been asked for further copies and am happy that with the co-operation of 'Le Bureau' of Lewes, it has been possible to reproduce this edition at a favourable price.

SINCE 1975 the author has lived in the cottage at Chiddingly that was the home of her great great grandfather, John-Clifford Russell, the village boot and shoemaker. These verses are a tribute to the family connection and the 200 year history of the house.

TODAY AT CORDWAINER'S

Who set that brick just there?
Little did he know, that come two hundred years or so,
It would carry through its core
An ambient glow, to flood the gilt-framed vision
of my Victorian ancestor.

Who put that board down there?
Solid plain flooring which at one time supported
A jumble of small bodies against the night's cold.
Little did he know, that come two hundred years or so,
A modern stair would thrust through those very bones,
To expose the intimacy of that foetid hold.

Who put that tile on there?
With wooden peg and mallet.
Little did he know that come two hundred years or so
The blushing apples in the void below
Would be ousted by a metal tree,
Which would shed its fruit in a box below.

Who put his initials there?
It was to the door at the top of the old stair.
Little did he know that come two hundred years or so,
It would keep privy to a wondrous place,
Where water would gush in steamy bursts,
Without the benefit of copper furnace.

Who put that casement there?
In Georgian style symmetrical to its fellow.
Little did he know, that come two hundred years or so,
The riven tube that now assaults the frame
Would bring the whole world into the compass
of that cottage niche,
By finger dial and cradled earpiece.
He could not know, who put them so . . .
José Loosemore

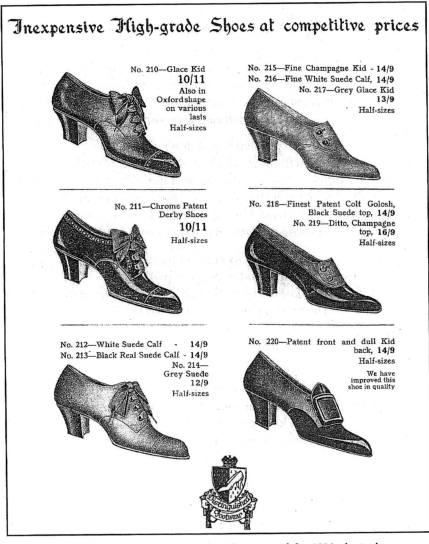

Inexpensive High-grade Shoes at competitive prices

No. 210—Glace Kid
10/11
Also in
Oxford shape
on various
lasts
Half-sizes

No. 215—Fine Champagne Kid - **14/9**
No. 216—Fine White Suede Calf, **14/9**
No. 217—Grey Glace Kid
13/9
Half-sizes

No. 211—Chrome Patent
Derby Shoes
10/11
Half-sizes

No. 218—Finest Patent Colt Golosh,
Black Suede top, **14/9**
No. 219—Ditto, Champagne
top, **16/9**
Half-sizes

No. 212—White Suede Calf - **14/9**
No. 213—Black Real Suede Calf - **14/9**
No. 214—
Grey Suede
12/9
Half-sizes

No. 220—Patent front and dull Kid
back, **14/9**
Half-sizes
We have
improved this
shoe in quality

An Albion Russell and Son advertisement of the 1920s featuring
'distinguished footwear'.

AUTHOR'S NOTE

WHY he chose me I do not know, but I feel that John-Clifford Russell singled me out to tell the story of what led, among other matters, to the formation of a business with a national household name.

At first I jibbed. I was only mildly interested in the intriguing subject of forebears. Although my father, Albion Percy Smith, was born and bred in Sussex and adored his county, he had been away from it for many years by virtue of his occupation as a seafarer. When in faraway places he often wrote and dreamed of home and on his infrequent bouts of leave – he was once away for nine months, leaving my mother to cope with two small daughters in London – he told us tales of his childhood in Rotherfield, where he was born in 1890. Albion Percy was only four when his father, Frederic Smith, died in 1894 at the age of forty-four leaving his mother with a family of nine children.

I never knew my grandmother Lydia Jane. She died in 1915 while my father was at sea. There was a photograph, which I was shewn, of a severe-faced woman in bombazine with a high-collared tight bodice, one hand delicately touching her throat, the other hand poised on the splats of a bobbin-turned chair. In the background some highly unlikely Arcadian scene suggested a far more opulent setting than the photographer's studio.

Father's recollection of village minutiae of the 'Ebenezer Wickens leg bore a huge callous due to continually hitting it whilst working on harness making' variety was prodigious and fascinating. However, his reminiscences unfortunately did not include important information on my grandma and poor dead grandpa. The only direct reference to grandma's relations was father's statement that her family had been connected to a shoemaking firm which was in business in what he described as 'quite a big way'.

We were well acquainted with several of my father's brothers and sisters and kept in touch throughout the years. His youngest sister,

Bessie, who was born in 1894 after her father died, lived at Brighton during her married life.

One of my fondest childhood memories was going to stay with Aunt Bessie where my sister Olive and I were allowed to be up and out after dark during the season to see the illuminated trams thunder along the Steine and sway perilously past the Royal Pavilion.

When Aunt Bessie died in the 1960s there was, among her effects, a small shagreen diary. It was written in 1849 at Uckfield by my great grandmother, Lydia Jane's mother, also a Jane. Oh! how confusing the Victorians were in their name choosing.

This Jane, daughter of Thomas and Martha Norman, had been born in Hellingly, near Hailsham in 1812; had married George Taylor in Brighton in 1831; and was widowed at the age of twenty-seven. She re-married in 1843 at Uckfield and her second husband was my great grandfather, George Clifford Russell.

In the following pages I have endeavoured to record all the information and dates which have any bearing on the related families which have contributed to the emergence of *A Story of Sussex Shoemakers*. To avoid over-burdening the general reader with a huge amount of factual detail it is confined to the appendices, where it might be of assistance to other family historians anxious to study Sussex-based 'names'.

Family descent, after the first generation from 'Heads', will be found at the end. Prominence has been given to the branches connected with shoe-making and followed by the associated families whose business and/or social lives were intertwined, albeit in various other occupations. Anyone claiming kinship is most welcome to the many photographs and documents of record which I have collected in twenty years of research.

José Loosemore
Chiddingly

8

1

THE QUEST BEGINS

MY great grandmother's diary was hand written in indelible pencil and the first thing I had to do was to get it transcribed. Names of people and places I had never heard of emerged from the greyness of the pencil script.

January 29 1849 – Albion married Miss S J Willard of Lewes.

Who was Albion? (It was my father's first name). This entry, I later discovered, was very propitious in the family story I was to unravel.

February 25 – George walked to Chiddingly.

Where was Chiddingly and why did he go there?

January 14 – Grandma and Alice dined with us off goose.

Which or whose grandma and who was Alice?

January 18 – Mr Tickner smoked a pipe and talked of letting us the house.

Which house or shop and who was Mr Tickner?

February 14 – George walked to Chiddingly to hear a sermon for the Jews.

Walked? Chiddingly is some ten miles from Uckfield. . .

April 26 – John swallowed a button.

Who was he and did it do any damage?

I was determined to discover the identity of all the people mentioned and the places named in the diary. On a map of Uckfield I marked: *Coopers Green, Grant's Hill. The Rocks, Buxted Park.*

Gradually things fell into place. George Clifford Russell had married his first wife, Jane Taylor, a thirty-one year old widow, in

London Road, Uckfield.

On the left is George Clifford Russell's first shop in Uckfield High Street, shown here occupied by draper, Richard Hollyman, and possibly rebuilt by him *c* 1860.

Uckfield in 1843. He had started a boot-making business in the town three years previously in premises at the top of High Street, opposite Copthall and near to the former Cottage Hospital. The shop was subsequently acquired by a draper, Richard Hollyman, and was known as Leicester House. Until quite recently it was the Uckfield garage premises of Barnard and Brough.

Whether George used the Golden Boot as a shop sign on these premises is not known but when he moved to a shop he had rented from William Tickner, 'opposite the Maidens Head' the boot appears as a logo in his advertisement in the *Uckfield Visitors' Guide* of 1869. These premises, which he was to buy, complete with furniture, from Tickner in July 1849, became 168 High Street when shops and houses were numbered. Jane recorded the two transactions in her diary. On January 18 is the entry: *'Mr. Tickner smoked a pipe and talked of letting us the house'*, and on July 25: *'Mr Tickner and Mr Holman* (a land surveyor) *came to settle, dear George signed agreement for house and furniture and paid ten shillings'*.

The ten shillings was presumably for the agreement.

Jane died from pulmonary tuberculosis in 1850. She had borne George two children, first a son, John Norman, and then, in 1849, the year of the diary, a daughter, Lydia Jane, who was my grandmother. She died in 1915.

Jane was described in census returns as a schoolmistress. Of my grandmother's birth she wrote in her diary on September 2 1849:

'God be praised for all his mercies to me. He blessed me with a good labour in giving birth to a fine girl . . .

But after this happy event her health deteriorated and she was often confined to the house although on *'good days'* she went to church or other meetings, and *'walked in J Cameron's nursery grounds'* with her friend, *'Mrs Mathews, who kept the Berlin and Fancy Wool Shop in the High Street'*.

The diary shows that the Russells were friends with a local auctioneer, T S Markwick and his wife, and a *'Miss Mannington called often'*. She was the proprietress of a young ladies boarding academy in the town, perhaps the one where Jane was a schoolmistress.

The family patronised John Turner's provision shop. From there, on one occasion, Jane purchased *'a box of French plums'* and another entry records that she *'bought a flead off Mrs Peerless of Hurstwood Farm which weighed 14filbs'*.

The next day, March 16 – *'Fine morn. Busy boiling up flead. Bought half a hogshead from Mrs P.'*

On April 19 – *'Mr. Prince the surgeon called to see son John aged four. Mrs Prince called as well, bringing the two pills which her husband had not only prescribed but made up in his own dispensary'*.

Little John was obviously very poorly as Mr Prince called on several days in succession, bringing on April 23 *'a box of pills'* although he found the child *'a little better'* and this pattern continued until May 12 when Jane wrote: *'John better, went to school.'*

Charles Leeson Prince was Uckfield's Registrar of Births and Deaths and also a noted amateur astronomer and meteorologist with an observatory in his garden. His father was also a medical man and the families lived in a house behind the High Street, opposite the Maiden's Head Inn. The Prince family owned the shop and a house fronting the High Street into which George Clifford Russell moved when he left the premises higher up the hill opposite Copthall.

Mrs Pentecost was another neighbour who called or was called upon. Her husband, Thomas, was a leathercutter and he would have had close ties with George, whose Golden Boot shop was evidently prosperous as he had, by this time, seven men and several apprentices working for him.

'Grandma' of earlier diary mention, I had discovered by this time was none other than Mary Russell, the mother of John-Clifford Russell and grandmother of George. The census of 1841 shows her established in Uckfield with her daughter, Alice. *Pigot's Directory* of later date describes her as a schoolmistress and lists her again in 1861, but this red herring has been disposed of because Mary Russell had died by 1857. Presumably the information about her had not been removed from the printed page.

Mary lived in the Elizabethan house which fronts the High Street, by the side of Olives yard. Here she boarded several apprentices for her grandson, George's, business, among them William Tickner from whom George bought his house. It may have been that the house in question was Olives, and that George Russell installed his grandmother there and Tickner remained in his own home as a lodger.

Olives is an unusual name for a house. However, some light is shed on how it came to be so called by this entry in *Uckfield Visitors' Guide* of 1869:

'The visitor will not fail to notice, on leaving the station, the picturesque old house close to the bridge. Farther up on the High Street he will observe, over the shop of Fisher, the harness-maker, a couple of early English capitals, bearing between them the inscription:

OLIVE
MLXV

'This fragment was dug up some years since, in the garden behind the house, which is an old one . . . The sculpture is no doubt genuine, but the inscription which is evidently modern, appears to have been executed by some clever mason surnamed Olive – a name which is not uncommon in the locality. . .'

Jane died on January 17 – the same date that she was born. She was only thirty eight and her coffin was placed in the tomb of her uncle, John Pocock, in St Nicholas churchyard, Brighton. He had been clerk to the Chapel Royal from 1795 to 1808 and clerk to the parish church from 1808 to 1846.

The last few months of her journal record her worsening health and her concern for her new child:

November 23 – Poor I, very poorly, baby fretting for the breast.

December 3 – Mary Heaver engaged to come, baby and all, to give my baby the breast.

December 14 – Sarah Holland came from Brighton as wet nurse. Had no milk, gave her a fair trial.

December 15 – Sent Holland back again, paid her fare both ways.

Less than two years later George Clifford remarried, having in the meantime taken on a housekeeper, one Miriam Ellis, to help care for his orphaned daughter. His son John, now aged six, did not appear in the census and was probably boarded elsewhere. George's new wife was Joanna Anable of Crich, Derbyshire, who he married in St Mary's church, Nottingham on December 11 1851. By her he had three other children – Joseph Clifford, Harriett and Elizabeth Ann.

George died in 1874 and was buried beneath the giant cedar that overhung the family plot in Holy Cross churchyard at Uckfield. He was laid to rest beside his second wife, Joanna, who had died, aged forty six, from injuries sustained from a fall in the snow on February 3 1865, and their daughter, Harriet, who had died at Eastbourne on July 16 1873.

The hurricane that caused such devastation in southern England in October 1987 uprooted the cedar tree. It crashed down and shattered the tombstone but part of the stone was undamaged and now lies on the turf opposite the old school and the wall of Belmont Lane.

In Fond Remembrance of
HARRIETT,
THE AFFECTIONATE DAUGHTER OF G. C. RUSSELL,
OF UCKFIELD,
Who died at St. John's Villa, Eastbourne, July 16, 1873,
AGED 18 YEARS.
THE FLOWER FADETH.

After George's death the sons of his two marriages, John Norman and Joseph Clifford, worked together as 'Russell and Co' at 168 High Street for eight years. Then John Norman moved away to Hastings and by 1884 was living and working in Horsham. After spending a

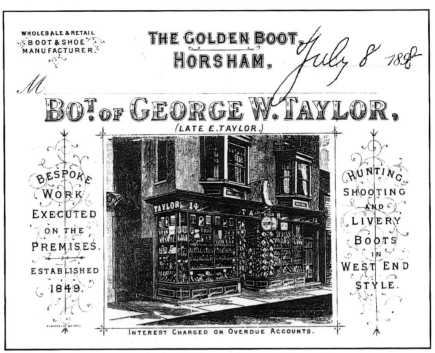

WHOLESALE & RETAIL
BOOT & SHOE
MANUFACTURER.

THE GOLDEN BOOT,
HORSHAM,

July 8 1898

M

BOT OF GEORGE W. TAYLOR,
(LATE E. TAYLOR.)

BESPOKE
WORK
EXECUTED
ON THE
PREMISES.

ESTABLISHED
1849.

HUNTING,
SHOOTING
AND
LIVERY
BOOTS
IN
WEST END
STYLE.

TAYLOR 14

INTEREST CHARGED ON OVERDUE ACCOUNTS.

A July 8 1898 billhead of the Golden Boot at 14 West Street, Horsham.

short time in Pulborough he returned to Horsham in 1889 to work with George W Taylor, a relative from his mother's side of the family. By 1907 he had his own premises at 44a Carfax, Horsham.

Like his mother, John Norman kept a diary, now in the possession of his granddaughter, Mrs Joy Holdsworth. In it he admits a preference for such outdoor pursuits as fishing to running a shoe shop and explains away his lack of success in business with the entry: *'Money goes out as fast as earned so got tired of keeping accounts'*.

After John Norman's departure the Uckfield business was carried on by Joseph Clifford. He had gained valuable management experience running the small shop George Clifford had opened at Maresfield and in his capable hands Russell and Co continued to flourish and to expand.

To what extent, and with what type of stock, can be seen from a most complimentary article in *Views and Reviews* published *c* 1895 by W T Pike of Brighton. It states:

14

'One of the most attractive looking trading premises in the town is the "Golden Boot" in which, under the able management of Messrs Russell and Co, a very successful and increasing business is carried on. Having been established over fifty years, it enjoys the distinction of being the leading house in the trade throughout the district.

'The stock consists of a large assortment of boots and shoes, court and dress shoes in great variety, football boots and requisites, shooting and rubber boots, while hunting and livery boots are made to order. . . The miscellaneous stock consists of gaiters, purses, portmanteaus and bags, which are made a specialty of . . . The business has so increased of late that the whole of the upstairs premises is used as a store and workroom, while behind the shop Messrs Russell have arranged a handsome fitting room, well carpeted and furnished, a convenience which must be appreciated by the many that visit their establishment.'

It was Joseph Clifford who supervised the third and last move made by the firm in Uckfield – to one of a row of shops built by Alfred Chilton

A golden boot, flanked by suitcases and hatboxes, appears above the fascia of 'the most attractive-looking trading premises in the town'

on part of the Old Grange estate. It was from this new shop, 162 High Street, that his wife, Ann, sent an order for cakes to Mrs Cruttenden at the Post Office, Southover, Lewes. The message on the postcard which shows a view of Uckfield High Street, reads:

'Please send by early afternoon train on Monday four 6d cakes 2 Chocolate 1 walnut 1 cherry. 6d worth rice cakes (small) and oblige. Mrs Russell High Street Uckfield.

In his reminiscences, entitled *Uckfield Fifty Years Ago* and published

in 1908, retired businessman David Wood mentions Russell and Co's third move and expresses his approval of the name – the Golden Boot:

'It is a good name Mr Russell, we hope it will be there for generations to come'.

This optimistic hope was not realised, however, because Joseph Clifford Russell died in 1934, at the age of eighty two. He was buried in Snatch Road cemetery, Uckfield, in the same grave as Ann, his wife, who had died in January the previous year.

A 1904 photograph of Joseph Clifford Russell.

The business was sold to a multiple shoe retailer, Milward and Son.

The third and last premises in Uckfield, and only 'Russell' is on the fascia of 162 High Street in the early 1900s.

16

2

TEA FOR THREE

JANE'S diary had proved a constant source of interest to me and I was intrigued by her references to a place called Chiddingly, as well as to the shop at Uckfield. In 1971 I was living in London with my first husband, Ken. My cousin, Joy Holdsworth, whose grandfather was also George Clifford Russell of Uckfield, wrote and told me that an Ernest Clifford Russell of Lewes, a bootmaker, had recently died and his will had been published.

There was an Ernest Clifford Russell and a Clifford Smith in the branches of our family tree, so might this man be a relative? The will was studied and it gave one private address – that of a Mrs Octavia Russell of Priory Crescent, Lewes. I wrote to her and received a courteous reply to the effect that she was indeed sister-in-law to the late Ernest C Russell; that her late husband Leslie had been very interested in his family tree; and that I would be better advised to make contact with the deceased's three sisters who lived in Hove.

Now here was a dilemma. How would these three maiden ladies react to a complete stranger making inquiries about the testator of a substantial will? However, the possibility of learning more of my grandmother's family spurred me on to write to them. In due course I received a telephone call from Miss Beatrice Russell. She said that from what I had briefly told them in my letter it was possible that we were related and shortly she and her sister, Edith, would be coming up to London. She suggested that I meet them in the tea lounge at Derry and Tom's department store.

'We will be wearing buttonholes of red flowers' wrote eighty three year old Beatrice in her letter to me confirming the appointment. I

The Russell sisters at Lyndhurst Road, Hove. Left to right: Winifred 1898-1983, Beatrice 1888-1982 and Edith 1902-1988.

approached the assignation with great excitement and entered the restaurant on the appointed day looking for a likely couple, who would probably be seated apart from other patrons but with a chair at the ready for me.

No need for red button holes. There sat two alert ladies and how like my father they were. I threaded my way between tables and said 'You must be the Misses Russell'.

Almost immediately the small table was swamped with photographs produced by both sides. Yes, their brother Ernest Clifford was the last remaining son of their father, Albion Russell.

'Albion' I almost shrieked,' that's my father's name and it is quite uncommon'.

'So your great grandfather, George Clifford, must be brother to our grandfather who was also Albion.'

From this moment on the Albion father and son were dubbed Albion One and Albion Two.

The father of brothers Albion and George Russell was therefore

John-Clifford Russell, who lived all his life at Chiddingly, a village near Hailsham. Jane's diary had confirmed this connection for she had written: *'George walked to Chiddingly to see his father'*.

Out of a capacious handbag, the second sister Edith produced a small postcard-sized wood-engraved print. It showed a rural scene featuring three cottages with a church spire in the background.

'This picture' she said 'was done by my grandfather, Albion, when he was sixteen and a half years old, and we have the wood-block at home'. It was dated and signed 'A Russell 1840'. The smallest of the three houses clearly had 'Russell' over the door.

'That was the shoe shop' said Miss Edith 'and the family lived in the cottage next door.'

By this time the tea had arrived and we hastily cleared a space for the teapot and cakes, conscious of the glances of nearby shoppers who were fascinated by the goings on at this rather unsuitable rendezvous.

I gazed at the print. 'So this is Chiddingly', I said, using the 'lye' pronounciation.

'Have you ever been there, or heard of it?' asked Beatrice.

Sixteen year old Albion Russell's wood engraving of Chiddingly in 1840, showing the shop bearing the name 'Russell' near the church.

19

'I have only read about it in Jane Russell's diary', I replied, pointing to the little volume on the tea table.

'Quite extraordinary', said Beatrice, 'usually people who don't know the place pronounce it 'Chiddinglee'.

'I should like to ask you one more thing', I said. 'Are your Russells anything to do with the firm of Russell and Bromley?'

'We ARE Russell and Bromley', said Edith quietly drawing herself up in her chair.

It was their grandfather, Albion One, whose daughter married a Bromley, and my great grandfather, George Clifford Russell, was Albion's elder brother. The sisters graciously gave me the copy of the little print and we parted company with promises on both sides to meet again.

I could hardly contain myself as I returned to my home at Merton Park, taking sneak peeks at the postcard now in my possession, as the train rattled down the Northern Line, through Kennington to Morden station.

3

A PLACE CALLED CHIDDINGLY

MY next resolve was to visit this place called Chiddingly and with my sister, Olive, we made the trip in 1972. I parked the car at Place Farm corner, outside the house known as The Place in the seventeenth century when it was the home of the illustrious Jefferay family, and we walked up the village street.

Would the cottages on Albion's wood-engraving still be there? My eye caught sight of a beautiful red rose which thrust its way up an interesting Georgian house-front which abutted the highway. Halfway up the wall my attention was drawn to a plaque which could just be observed between the rose branches.

'Olive, I've found something interesting. Look at this plaque. It says J-C R 1839. '

The initials were obviously those of John-Clifford Russell. When we stood back a little way we could see that the house formed the third of the terrace of three, which Albion One had shewn in his wood engraving.

There to the left was the smallest house which had at one time carried the name Russell on its fascia; the cottage in which the considerable family overflowed from the

21

'shop' cottage to the middle one and finally to the end house of much bigger proportions than the other two. This one, I was to learn, J-C R had built to accommodate his shoemaking business, to house his workforce, stable his pony and traps and provide store rooms for the stock of equipment needed in an expanding business.

It was some months later that news reached me that the former shop/cottage was going on the market. Ken and I decided that it would be exciting to see inside this little house, so we got in touch with the agents and drove down once again to Chiddingly.

The two-up two-down cottage was built in about 1780 and was very small. It had a kitchen/scullery under a catslide roof, and faced south to the Downs. In recent years it had been used as a holiday home and apart from the addition of a shower and a WC at the end of the kitchen – there was no bathroom– the only hot water system was a small Sadia heater in the corner.

It was an historic find.

Ken looked at me quizzically.

'Yes, I know what you are going to say – how would you like to live here?'

'Well would you?' I said tentatively.

'It's very small 'he said defensively 'and then there is your work to be considered.'

Ken had recently taken early retirement when a massive reorganisation of his Croydon firm had resulted in computerised central buying and we both felt he needed a change.

'Well', I said, 'if the Greater London Council thinks I can do my job and live at this distance from town yes, I'd love to come and live here'.

At this moment I was sure that J-C R's shade was encouraging me to make this pronouncement. On the surface it was a very foolish decision. We had a delightful three-bedroom house in a semi-rural setting near Wimbledon, with a lovely garden which we both adored. True our children were by then away from home, but it would be necessary to sell most of the furniture of our London home, which would never have fitted into the small cottage.

On our way back to London we stopped off at the house agent's office. It was closed, so I hurriedly scribbled a note, which read:

'Please negotiate with the owners, my great great grandfather owned the cottages between 1821 and 1857', attached it to Albion's picture of Chiddingly, and popped it through the letterbox.

Back in town we awaited the outcome and were rewarded with a telephone call to say that the vendors were prepared to accept our offer. It came so swiftly that the enormity of our decision swept over us. Now we were faced with selling our own house. Naturally the owners wished the matter to be concluded rapidly. Could we do it? It was a bad time of the year, November, what if we could not sell? Then I had an idea.

The Russell sisters at Hove had spoken very warmly of their cousin Michael Bromley, then managing director of Russell and Bromley. Even if we cannot have the cottage, I temporised, perhaps the firm would like to save it for personal reasons – or staff use as a holiday home. So I wrote to Michael, 'as one descended from John Clifford Russell of Chiddingly. . . would your firm care to save this historic cottage?

As our great great grandfathers were brothers I presumed to add, 'if you do not require it for your own use, would the firm purchase it and hold it for us until we sell our present house?'

It was probably impudent, but to our everlasting joy I received a very encouraging letter from Michael Bromley. He would like to meet Ken and me and then he would discuss my request with his fellow directors. We met at our London house and in a remarkably short time later, we received a further letter. The company did not require the property, but were willing to purchase and hold the cottage against us selling our house in town. R and B did this on very generous terms which included a clause that only if it took longer than six months to conclude the sale of the Merton Park house would they impose a modest interest on the loan.

By January 1975 a desultory procession of people had answered our advertisement through the property agent. We did not like the people who kept telling us what they would tear out, alter, dig up or otherwise vandalise – should they take the property. It was beastly, but if they had come back we would have felt bound to sell.

We were sitting at home one miserable evening early in the New Year, when about 9pm the telephone rang.

'Is your house on the market?'

'Yes, when do you want to see it?'

'Could we come now?' said the voice,

'Er – if you wish, but you won't see the garden,' I said lamely.

Half an hour later a young couple arrived. We liked them. They did not say anything about ripping this or that out. They drank a glass of sherry with us and left saying they would be in touch

'Aren't they nice,' I said to Ken 'but I don't suppose we'll hear any more from them'.

At 10 pm the telephone trilled.

'We're the people who came earlier.'

I was about to say – 'It's courteous of you to at least tell us you have decided against it', when Richard, the caller, said – 'We'll take it'.

'But you can't', I said. 'You haven't seen the garden yet'.

The Andersons were wonderful. They agreed to buy our furniture which we knew would not fit into the cottage at Chiddingly. They did not haggle over prices, which we thought had been pitched sensibly, and the whole business was settled within a few weeks – we had the key to our new home and they had the keys to our house. Several years on we called on Richard and Mary and found they were still using 'our' carpet and sitting room furniture.

The morning we had learned that our offer for the cottage at Chiddingly had been accepted I was at a Christmas Fair organised by Time and Talents of Bermondsey, an old established settlement which grew out of a Christian need to give support to the under-privileged inner city areas.

Giving her services as a reader of tea leaves on this occasion was a local celebrity, Julia Bygraves-Mahoney, a cousin of comedian Max Bygraves. When I arrived as one of the helpers, I was persuaded to let Julia tell my fortune – something I had steered clear of all my life.

'Go on, it's only a bit of fun' they said, and I succumbed.

I had taken the postcard print of Chiddingly by Albion One with me to the fair but had not had time before seeing Julia to show the card to anyone or talk about the possibility of leaving London. It was safely tucked into my handbag awaiting an opportunity to tell my friends about our future plans.

I drank the obligatory cup of tea, Julia solemnly swirled the

A drawing by Leo Hardy of Chiddingly village as it is today.

residue around and placed the cup upside down in the saucer.

'I see a row of houses or, er – buildings. They are all joined together', she said. 'I see an old boot with its toe gaping open, that means good luck. I see a letter, it could be the figure seven, and the letter B is prominent. You have been very unsettled lately, but everything will come all right'.

I drew the postcard out of my bag.

'If I were to say that this very morning we have had news that we have been able to buy the small cottage on this postcard; that it is one of a terrace of three; and it was once the home of my great great grandfather, who was the village boot and shoemaker; that the people who made it possible are called Bromley; that the neighbour who informed me that the cottage was on the market is a Miss Bellamy; and the man in charge of the cottage in the absence of the owner is Baker what would you say ?'

'I saw it all in the teacup,' replied Julia Bygraves-Mahoney.

This redoubtable seer appears to have read the tea leaves with remarkable accuracy – with a couple of exceptions. We were musing some months later on the events which led us to Chiddingly. She was right about buildings 'all joined together', the old boot had great significance, but the figure seven, how did that fit in ?

'Mum', said my daughter Helen one day, 'what was the date that the Andersons called late one evening on the 'phone, just after Christmas, wasn't it January 7?'

She was right and then we discovered that it had taken exactly seven weeks for the whole business to be transacted – surely a record in house buying negotiations with three parties involved.

We invited Julia Bygraves-Mahoney down for a special weekend once we had settled in. By this time the figure of my great great grandfather had assumed an importance in our lives. My new-found

Russell cousins at Hove had supplied me with an interesting photograph of a portrait of him and I had begun to delve into parish records and those at the East Sussex Records Office in Lewes.

Julia knew nothing of my ancestors so I felt I would test her powers further. I showed her the photograph of John-Clifford Russell's portrait.

'Tell me', I said 'What does the picture tell you?'

She studied it carefully for several minutes and then said:

'He wasn't an ordinary sort of person, he was a "somebody"– and he was a very just man'.

John-Clifford Russell's portrait in oils.

'That is very interesting', I said and, in thanking her, added casually: 'The man who once owned the terrace of three cottages, including the one in which we are now, is the subject of the photograph'.

I secretly hugged to myself the knowledge that up in Chiddingly churchyard, John-Clifford Russell's tombstone bore the epithet 'the memory of the just is blessed. . .'

Julia knew nothing of this and had never been to Chiddingly until that weekend.

We set about the conversion of the little house, our aim being to make it habitable and bring it up to acceptable modern living standards without altering it more than necessary. The work took thirteen weeks, and at the end of the period we had gained one living room from two very small ones, converted one bedroom to an upstairs landing, added a south-facing bedroom by cutting into the catslide roof – it was sad to see this go but it was inevitable – and also got a bathroom out of the void over the old lean-to kitchen.

We were back in the house by Christmas 1975. It has always felt friendly, as if inhabited by warm spirits. I am sure great great grandfather's family had welcomed the return of a descendant almost 120 years after the last Russell left, when the houses had been sold in 1857.

4

MARY RUSSELL - THE MISSING YEARS

IT was at Chiddingly in 1791 that Mary, a young girl of fifteen and a half, bore a son. She was one of twelve children of Robert and Ann Russell, a couple so poor that they were unable to pay the 3d tax levied at this period, and suffered the indignity of an exemption mark of 'P' against their name in the parish register.

To cope with the spectre of poverty, at least two of their daughters were 'put out', Mary to Joseph Willard, and Martha to Sam Holman, as was a son, William. That is to say that other families took these children into their homes, and were provided with an annual sum from the Churchwardens and Overseers of the Poor towards their keep.

Mary was first sent to a Mr Willard of Burchetts, Chiddingly, for a year from March 1787 'and he to have £2 with her and the Parish to cloth her'. The contract was renewed for a further year until 1789. Where did she go after this? All that is known is that she became pregnant and was delivered of an illegitimate son on May 7 1791.

Now things get complicated. In Chiddingly parish records for 1791 is the entry:

'Russell. John son of Robert and Ann, born 22 May'

AND

'Russell. John son of Mary Russell baseborn 7 May'

Both were baptised on August 7 that year. What an extraordinary coincidence that mother and daughter should both produce sons only a few weeks apart and give both children the same baptismal name. In all the documents I have come across this 'Uncle John' has only been mentioned twice, once when he was 'removed' with his parents, Robert and Ann, from Chiddingly to Hellingly by the parish officers in 1792, and again when his name appeared in a document in my possession as a beneficiary under his nephew, John-Clifford Russell's will.

Mary Russell, after the birth of John-C Russell, may have gone into service in one of the grander or more substantial houses of the time. There were several in the area – Pekes Manor, and Burchetts, Friths, Shirleys and The Hale, all yeomen's houses. And then, of course, there was Chiddingly Place, the former Elizabethan manor house of the Jefferay family, which by this time had been demoted to a farm house in the ownership of the Guy family. One of the wings of this old house had become a great barn which showed, by its blocked up mullions and the remains of a fireplace high on the upper wall, that it had been part of an E shaped house, built in this way to honour Queen Elizabeth 1. Finally there was Chiddingly Park, a former seat of the Sackvilles, which survived as Park Farm, occupied by Thomas Funnell in the 1800s. It was his descendant, John Funnell, who took on the young bastard, my J-C R.

What happened to Mary after she bore her son in Chiddingly in 1791 remained a mystery until my cousin Joy found her name in a document in East Sussex Records Office in Lewes. It was on a bond drawn up between her and the churchwardens and overseers of Framfield in 1819 'to indemnify the Parochial Officers of that Parish of the charge of a female child, Alice'. Mary Russell was bound in the sum of £100 – quite a small fortune in those days.

The pages of Jane Russell's 1849 diary came immediately to mind – 'Grandma and Alice dined with us of goose' and 'Grandma and Alice tea'ed with us'. Yes, there was the evidence of the birth of a second illegitimate child. It was backed up by the entry in the Uckfield census returns for 1851 which reads:

'Olives. Mary Russell aged 75, school-mistress, born Chiddingly. Alice Russell, age 29, school-mistress, natural daughter, born Framfield'.

Several years later a third possible child emerged, but had been born before Alice in 1798. He was 'found' in the International

Genealogical Index (Mormon index) at Lewes, born out of wedlock to a Mary Russell at Framfield. Why did I feel that we should or even want to claim him?

1) Because a genealogist of my acquaintance, Peter Ferguson, found, in the census of 1821, a George Russell living at Olives, High Street, Uckfield.

2) Because John-Clifford Russell named a 'George Russell' as a sponsor to his son Julius at the child's baptism in 1819. This young man would have been about twenty years of age at the time.

3) This George Russell was in the census of 1855 as being in business in Uckfield as Russell and (Thomas) Wallis, Drapers.

In his early years Mary Russell's little boy was cared for and nurtured in the village of his birth until the dire circumstances of the times forced his mother to part with him.

The overseers' records show that in 1803, when he was twelve years old, John Clifford was 'put out', as his mother had been before him, with Mr John Funnell of Park Farm Chiddingly and this arrangement lasted until 1804 'and he to have with him £2 12 0d and the Parish to Cloth him.' The following year he was again 'put out', this time to Mr Richard Hicks, 'the mother to Cloth him and he is to have £2 with him'.

From then until manhood his formative years are pure conjecture. He must have learned to read and write, but whether it was at the knee of the scholarly Richard Lower, schoolmaster, cartographer, and father of Mark Anthony, historian and antiquarian, whose family and schoolhouse were at the neighbouring hamlet of Muddles Green, or at the grammar school in Uckfield, perhaps paid for by his elusive father, is not known.

Did John Funnell of Park Farm introduce the young John Russell to Mr William Thorpe as a likely young lad for his shoemaking business in The Street? The two men were probably related through Mary, William's first wife.

All attempts to find apprentice indentures to confirm that young John Russell entered shoemaking in this way have so far proved unsuccessful. It is possible that William Thorpe knew who the young boy's father was and was ready to welcome him into his home and family and to teach him the craft of a cordwainer. In all events, John

An 1838 wood engraving by Albion Russell, of the church in which his parents were married.

Russell in due time courted William's youngest daughter, Jane, who was ten years older than her betrothed.

They were married at Chiddingly on August 24, 1812. They anticipated their wedding vows as the first of their six children, a girl Harriet, was born in November that year. The marriage certificate reads:

'John Russell and Jane Thorpe, both of this Parish, in the presence of William Thorpe, Phyllis Thorpe, Richard Thorpe and Harriet Thorpe'.

Where were the Russells? Not even his mother, Mary, seems to have attended the ceremony.

For some reason, just after his marriage John Russell added 'Clifford' to his signature. In 1815 he signed the register as 'John-Clifford Russell' when his eldest son, my great grandfather, was baptised George Clifford Russell and he is recorded as a member of the parish vestry and as the village 'Land Tax Assessor to George IV' as Mr J-C Russell.

As it was fairly unusual at this period to be given a second Christian name, I thought it might be of some help in tracing the identity of his father. I noted this recurring inclusion of the 'Clifford' name in later family members. My Uncle Jack from Rotherfield was christened 'Clifford Smith', George Clifford Russell of Uckfield called his son by his second marriage 'Joseph Clifford' and there are at least half-a-dozen other descendants who received this name as a second appendage, including three who also took the name 'John' as a first name. Would this be the clue to help in my search for the putative father of John-Clifford Russell?

There were many red herrings in the absorbing quest for John-Clifford's father. Over the years I followed every clue. My first steps were guided by a descendant of Albion Two – his son Arthur Leslie Russell, brother to the Russell sisters of Hove. Sadly I never met him as he died some time before I became acquainted with my Hove cousins.

Leslie had obtained some information which led him to believe that Mary Russell's child of 1791 had been fathered by a 'Lord de Clifford'. This wisp of conjecture was fortified for me when I discovered that Peakes or Pekes Manor in Chiddingly had in the 1900s come into the possession of the Honourable Terence Bourke, son of the 7th Earl of Mayo. But I had to 'cancel the coronet' when I found that although the 21st Baron Edward de Clifford had indeed married a daughter of the 3rd Earl of Mayo, and she was named Mary, the marriage was childless. He died at Brighton in 1832, aged sixty five, after which the barony fell into abeyance for the fourth time.

There was, too, the family story that J-C.R's mother was sufficiently endowed by the father of her child, so that the boy was eventually able to establish himself as a bootmaker in Chiddingly. However, I believe that this was due to John being a beneficiary of his father-in-law, William Thorpe, and his own ability to succeed by hard work and fair business dealings. Did not the epitaph on his tombstone proclaim: 'the memory of the just is Blessed'?

Following my arrival in Chiddingly, I had been told that there were no more documents available in the parish's keeping other than registers which I had already seen. I employed a genealogist from Lewes and one from Bristol, as I knew a Lady de Clifford had died at Henbury where she had a residence, and I was eventually assured that all relevant Poor Law records, overseer's accounts and apprenticeship indentures had been perused but no trace could be found of

John-C Russell. 'In any case,' it was added 'the likelihood of your being able to trace an illegitimate child are slim indeed.'

However, I did find something. Under Overseer's Accounts, in splendid copperplate, were the very details I was seeking.

> 'John Clifford. Put out to Mr John Funnell from the 25th of March 1804 and he is to have with him £2 12. 0 and the parish to clothe him.'

The reference is to 'John Clifford' – the name 'Russell' is not mentioned – but yes, the boy 'put out' was the son of Mary Russell as other family evidence proved. Although interesting this did not give me the great leap forward I had anticipated, although it confirmed my view that the name Clifford was of paramount importance in my search for John's father.

Quite fortuitously, some seventeen years later, I discovered who John's father was. The then chairman of Chiddingly Parish Council, Colonel Andrew Weldon, knowing my interest in the history of the locality, showed me a list of documents relating to Chiddingly that had been deposited in the county archives by an officer of the parish council some years previously. Almost on the first page, under the title 'Warrants for the Arrest of Putative Fathers of Bastards' Ref.Page 292 15/3 I read:

> 'John Clifford of Rolvenden in Kent, miller, for the male bastard delivered on the 7th May 1791 of Mary Russell of Chiddingly.'

Although I now knew who John's father was I had yet to learn more of John Clifford, miller of Rolvenden. Did he, perhaps, pay for the schooling of his bastard son?

And was the father of Alice, born 1819, the same man who was responsible for Mary's first child?

I am inclined to think not. John-C Russell in his will, drawn up in 1845, left a guinea each to his aunts and uncles on his mother's side. Seven of them survived to claim it in 1851. However, his half-sister, Alice, and his mother, who, after all, was only fifteen and a half years his senior and outlived him by some eight years, are not mentioned in the will.

There was also this shadowy character called George Russell who was born illegitimately to a Mary Russell at Framfield in 1798 and was, according to the census of 1821, living with 'our' Mary Russell at Olives, High Street, Uckfield.

These are questions to which I may not gain answers, for lack of time and opportunity, even if such records exist. The discovery of the possible answers must be left to, one hopes, a future family historian.

The miller of Rolvenden has slipped as quietly out of focus as his entrance was manouevred into this story by the cryptic details which a great great grand-daughter in 1991 was able to confirm from a fragile parchment document in the muniments room at The Maltings in Lewes.

5

THE THORPE CONNECTION

WILLIAM THORPE, the head of an extensive family, was a person of importance in Chiddingly. He owned four acres of land, bought from David Guy of the Place Farm, and is believed to have built his two cottages in The Street around 1780.

The Thorpes originated in Surrey in the fourteenth century and came to Sussex by way of East Grinstead, Ifield and Buxted. In 1731 a Benjamin Thorpe married Ann Samsun by licence at Hastings and moved to Chiddingly. The couple had eight children, the youngest of which was William, born in 1747. He married Mary Funnell in Chiddingly church on November 20 1772, and they had six children, the youngest being Jane, John-Clifford Russell's bride-to-be.

When Mary died William re-married. Ann Barrow became his second wife in 1784 and by her he had eight more children.

With all these offspring, four of whom became cordwainers, why did William Thorpe chose J-C R to inherit his Chiddingly shoemaking business and the two cottages? Was it because his son-in-law chose to stay in the village with him while his own sons moved away to set up on their own?

His eldest son, William, who was born in 1776, had businesses in Hellingly and Horsebridge, near Hailsham; John, born in 1779, went off to Horsham; Richard, born 1787, set up as a cordwainer in Ashford, Kent and his youngest son, George, eventually moved to Battle where he set up business in 1819 at 14, High Street and later premises next door, where his descendants are to be found to this day

Rachael Thorpe, wife of Warren Homan Thorpe, pictured in 1972 outside 14 High Street, Battle where George Thorpe of Chiddingly started in business.

trading as B H Thorpe and Company.

The present proprietors, Wendy Campbell and Jeremy Thorpe, are George's great great grandchildren They are members of a fascinating family whose paths in life have taken them into the Church, the Law, coach-building, farming, accountancy and estate agency.

When George's son, George Archibald Thorpe, was nineteen he was set up by his father as a shoemaker/retailer at 22 George Street in Old Town, Hastings. On September 10, 1857, he married Emma Homan, daughter of the one-time head of the wholesale bootmakers' factors, Homan and Hearn, and they had ten children.

It was with George Archibald that the first link in the chain that led to Russell and Bromley was forged. He was mayor of Hastings from 1874 to 1875 and again in 1887, the year of Queen Victoria's golden jubilee. His civic duties would have brought him into contact with fellow council member, Alderman John Roger Bromley, whose son, George Frederick, was apprenticed to Albion One at Lewes. The firm of Russell and Bromley was born out of his marriage to Albion's daughter, Elizabeth.

His half-uncle, John Thorpe, became the 'father' of several branches of the inter-married families who colonised the trading district of Horsham, namely West Street and Carfax, in the early nineteenth century. It was his son, also a John, who angered and upset the shop workers at Horsham by opposing any reduction in opening hours. In spite of protests he and his fellow traders, Stepney and Angus, kept their shops open and fully staffed until 9pm in the summer months, and it was not until 1845 that legislation forced them to close an hour earlier in both winter and summer.

One of the documents given me by the Russell sisters at Hove was a lengthy indenture on parchment. It was drawn up in 1821 between John Russell, 'Cordwainer of Chiddingly' and his brother-in-law, John Thorpe, 'Cordwainer of Horsham'. The deed provided the means whereby payment of £200 could be made under the terms of William Thorpe's will, dated 1815, to his estate in consideration of the transfer of the cottages devised to John-C Russell.

The Golden Boot hangs proudly outside Russell's in West Street, Horsham, on this 1924 postcard.

Edward and José Loosemore outside Cordwainer's in the summer of 1997.

This is one of several incidents indicating the cordial relationship that existed between J-C R and his Thorpe relations. They were entwined both commercially and socially and the fact that William's business had passed by devise to a son-in-law did not seem to cause any problem.

It was the 1821 indenture which led Ken and me to change the name of our house to Cordwainer's. It had been on the market as Thorne Cottage – a name that did not seem to be of relevance except that at one time the two cottages had appeared on some documents as Thorpe's Cottages. Perhaps 'Thorpe' had been mis-pronounced over the years and ended up as 'Thorne'?

A cordwainer is a bootmaker – one who works in fine leather (from Cordova in Spain) – not to be confused with a cobbler who only mends shoes. It seemed to be a fitting choice of name as the parchment which set J-C R on the road to prosperity describes the two men who were parties to the deed as cordwainers, as was also William Thorpe who owned the cottages up to his death in 1819.

6

THE CHIDDINGLY SHOEMAKER

BY 1821 John and Jane Russell were the owners of a thriving boot and shoemaking business in The Street. They had six children. Their first was Harriet, born in October 1812, the next was my great grandfather, George Clifford, born in 1815, then Charlotte 1817, Julius 1819, Albion 1821 and finally Jane in 1824.

They appeared to have been relatively healthy, only poor Charlotte dying in her seventeenth year. John was so pleased with his brood that he wrote, under the words 'grounds for exemption' in a Militia List of November 3 1824, the verse:

> If any exemption I hope to obtain
> I think it must be from my juvenile train
> For lo! I am blest with the greatest of joys!
> Having three healthy Girls and as many pert Boys

He addressed the lines to his friend, another cordwainer named Thomas Reed, 'from Reed's House by the Gun'.

Reed replied in similar vein:

Friend Russell,
> I fain would exempt you from serving the king,
> From blood and all that kind of trouble;
> But this I assure you – your juvenile string
> Won't do it – e'en tho' it were double!

> Yet this I will tell – yes, the world shall all know it
> The great and the small – low and high
> A Husband – A Father – A Friend – and A Poet
> May be found in the Vil. Chiddingly

*You will give me credit when I say I hate flattery. But I will not hesitate to say that the return you made is the best composition (for the subject) I ever saw written, and as to poetic merit may well compete even with Wm. Dine himself – not to the exclusion of Thos. Robt. Reed !!!

Shall insert it verbatim in the Militia List
4 Nov 1824

He folded the paper into an envelope shape, addressed and posted it to 'The Bard of the Vil. Chiddingly, Mr. J-C.Russell.'

The William Dine named in the footnote of Reed's reply, was at the time parish clerk of Chiddingly and known for his versifying. In 1771 he published a slim volume entitled *Poems on Several Occasions*.

I too had my fun on reading the exchange of verses between John Russell and Thomas Read and penned 'some *Parallel Lines* written after reading John-Clifford Russell's *Grounds for Exemption* published in the Militia List 1824' on all that had led to our coming to Sussex and the cottage. Here they are:

Cousin Bromley.

> Old J-C R's smiling in Chiddingly Street,
> He has waited a long time his family to meet,
> At last to his cottage - no 'juvenile train'
> But children of children of children again.

> The callers were several, all scions of the stock,
> From Hove Miss Bea Russell from Albion One's flock,
> His brother, George Clifford, was well represented
> By Albion P Smith (whose mother was Russell)

> As for Beatrice and Albion, now 'pert' eighty pluses
> They are both great grandchildren of John-Clifford Russell.
> Cousins Josephine Davis and V Russell Young,
> Joy Holdsworth of Otford and Olive Thornton,

> All gathered together with Jo's daughter, Helen,
> One of the many 'rear coaches' of J-C R's 'train',
> The Bromleys of <u>Bromley</u> (old coincidence again)
> Sent a Russell and Bromley – Michael Cornish by name.

> And now by the goodwill of Bromley cum Russell
> Ken and Josephine Davis will soon own this cottage.
> The year of revival – one nine seven five.
> Mary, mother of J-C, born one seven seven five.

> Two centuries separate these diverse occasions.
> A lot goes unanswered which cannot be reckoned,
> However, the wardens of Cordwainer's Cottage
> Will welcome descendants who visit the heritage.

> Perhaps in the haven of Sussex translation,
> John-Clifford's near presence will provide inspiration
> For a great great grand daughter the knot to untie
> Who <u>was</u> old John's father in the Vil Chiddingly?

John was twenty eight when William Thorpe died. In succeeding years the business he had inherited prospered and an eleven year old Chiddingly lad, John White, wrote in his diary, on August 28 1829: *'Mr Russell come and brought Mary-Ann's shoes and meshured* (sic) *me for some half boots.'*

In 1839 John-Clifford built an extension to the two cottages he had

Above: Albion
Russell's wood
engraving of the
cottages in The
Street before his
father added the
third house.

⁂

Left: A print of the
Jefferay monument
in Chiddingly church,
engraved by Albion
when he was
nineteen.

been left by his father-in-law. This addition, which had an arched central entrance to give access to the stables and outbuildings at the side, contained workshops and cutting, assembly and stock rooms.

In the census returns of the period he is described as a 'master shoemaker' and no doubt journeymen-shoemakers and apprentices worked for him in the new manufactory. It is said to have been one of the first places in Sussex to use mass methods of production in shoe-making – methods which Albion One later adopted and developed at Lewes in 1845.

John-Clifford took on a small shop – believed to have been on a site now occupied by houses in The Mews – at East Hoathly, the next village to Chiddingly. It was in premises owned by Matthew Martin in 1837, and he continued to trade there as well as Chiddingly until his death, as an account for £3 17s, directed to Baxter and Company of Lewes, publisher of the *Sussex Weekly Advertiser*, for the particulars of sale for the East Hoathly shop, shows.

Two of his sons followed their father's calling – George Clifford at Uckfield (see Chapter 1) and Albion at Lewes. But in his teens it seemed that Albion had other career ideas. As a child he had shown an aptitude for sketching and he may have spent some time with the printing firm of Baxter and Company at Lewes, possibly with a view to becoming a professional engraver. However, this is only surmise and cannot be confirmed as all Baxter's old records were destroyed by fire in the 1950s.

Wood blocks of Albion's engravings have survived. They are of Chiddingly church, the cottages in The Street before and after his father added the third house and a masterly engraving of the Jefferay monument for the Sussex Archeological Society.

In 1851 the executors of John's estate, (his sons George Clifford and Albion, and his nephew, John Thorpe Jnr) put the property at Chiddingly on the market. J-C R's widow, Jane, now seventy, had agreed to live with her youngest daughter, also Jane, who was married to John Andrews, a grocer and draper of Storrington in West Sussex. She died there in 1854 but was brought back to Chiddingly and buried in her husband's grave. Schoolmistress Naomi White, head of a 'young ladies academy' in Muddles Green and a relative of little George White, makes mention of the funeral in her diary of

1853-4: *'Mrs. J-C. Russell died at Storrington aged 72. Buried in our Church.'*

An advertisement in the *Sussex Weekly Advertiser* of March 18 1851 advised 'BOOT AND SHOE MAKERS, CAPITALISTS AND OTHERS' of the sale by private contract of the premises at Chiddingly which included the two cottages, one used as a shoemaker's shop, a coach-house, stable, large warehouse and outbuildings. It went on:

> 'The above property is freehold, brick and tile built, and is a very desirable spot for anyone in the trade, the late Mr Russell having for several years carried on a very extensive, respectable, and profitable business as a wholesale and retail boot and shoemaker, and a large business is now doing.
>
> 'The premises command a frontage abutting to the high road of 116 feet, are well supplied with excellent water, and are within about one minute's walk from the church. . . The garden is very productive, and well stocked with young and flourishing fruit trees, the late Mr Russell having been very particular in their selection. On the whole the property is well worthy of attention, either for investment or occupation'.

The disposal sale, as it transpired, did not materialise until November 3 1857 as there was some problem with a man called Davey, who agreed to buy, but then refused to go ahead with the contract because he was charged 'the poor rate' on it.

Eventually the vicar, the Reverend J H Vidal, purchased the whole lot for the sum of £335. When the same terrace was offered for sale in 1912 by the then owner, Henry Noakes, it sold for only £243 3s, including the stables. By 1975, when we bought the smallest cottage only, the price was £10,000, but there was an added piece of ground at the rear by this date.

The inventories of the contents have survived. In the Chiddingly warehouse, now called Yew Tree House, items included 'a glass case, 24ft of narrow shelving and 8ft of ditto'. In the upper workshop 'a stove and pipe, 5 seats, and 90 pairs of left and right lasts, pitch and rosin.' In the East Hoathly shop were twenty pairs of shoes and half-boots, one cupboard, one drawer and a stove.

There were a number of items not now included in the vocabulary of modern shoe retailing – such things as 'cloth boots, spring boots, velvet and cashmere boots, French clogs, kid operas, Bluchers and

Alberts' as well as pattens, the wooden clogs with iron rings attached to the base to raise the foot above the ever-present Sussex mud.

Among the items listed in laborious copperplate hand-writing on nine foolscap pages are the contents of the stable – 'one gilding (sic) pony, one light harness. . . Out of doors, near stable, one lump of manure' and 'one hive of bees, stack of meadow hay, five Southdown yews (sic).' In the domestic offices of washhouse, kitchen and cellar was 'one pork tub, one safe', in the coachhouse a 'light chaise cart, ditto cart etc.' The room by the stable contained 'one patent mangle, large oak chest', in one parlour was 'one ottoman and Kidderminster carpet.' There were four bedrooms, one with a half-tester bed.

'Two shops' brought the appraisal to a close at a sum of £599 17s 1d, 'attested by Sam Southerden, Auctioneer of Hailsham, Jan. 13th 1851' – a sum, at today's values, of more than £60,000.

Albion One's shop at 187-188 High Street, Lewes.
Photo by Edward Reeves, Lewes.

7

THE LEWES RUSSELLS

WHAT drew Albion back to shoemaking is not known but by 1848 he was running 'J. C. Russell and Son, Lewes Boot and Shoe Mart', the business his father had opened in premises rented from Baxters at 37 High Street, Lewes.

A flowery advertisement, typical of the period, appeared in the *Sussex Agricultural Express* of November 4 1848. It announced that:

'J. C. R. and Son have just received a large supply of the highly approved AMERICAN METALLIC RUBBER OVERSHOES for Ladies and Gentlemen, which are perfectly Impervious to wet and highly Elastic, and from their Light and Elegant appearance are far superior to any other kind of Goloshes now in use.

OBSERVE!—RUSSELL & SON, Wholesale and Retail Boot and Shoe Warehouse, Top of School Hill, Lewes.'

After the death of his father two years later Albion was on his own. By then his business address was 187-188 High Street, a big double fronted shop next to the Star Inn outside which, in 1555/7, seventeen Protestant martyrs were burnt at the stake for their beliefs. The shop, which bore the stark word 'RUSSELL' across its fascia, had, in earlier days, also been an inn and then a coffee house.

Albion was an enterprising young businessman. In 1854, during the Crimean War, he secured a contract to provide 500 pairs of boots at 6s 6d (32½ pence) a pair for the Russian prisoners of war housed in Lewes gaol. He had, by this time, a workforce of twenty-three men and six women, with workshops adjacent and to the rear of the Baxter printing works on School Hill.

Unlike his cousin, John Thorpe Jnr, who at Horsham opposed any reduction in shop opening hours, Albion Russell had his workers' welfare at heart. He supported the introduction of bank holidays and was one of the 'Merchants, Tradesmen, and others' who, in 1871, called upon 'the inhabitants of the town to close their respective business places and set apart Tuesday, December 26 as a public holiday'.

He became a person of influence and importance in the county town. By 1872 he was Joint High Constable with Robert Crosskey and to celebrate their appointments the two men hosted a luncheon in the county hall for 130 male guests – no women were present.

Among those attending this civic function was Alderman John Roger Bromley from Hastings. He did not know then that his son, George Frederick Bromley, would marry his host's daughter, Elizabeth, in two year's time. Alderman Bromley died in 1873 and so did not to witness the union of the two people who would give their joint names to a shoe company with a national reputation.

Albion installed the young couple in a branch shop in Seaside Road, Eastbourne and they ran it as part of

Albion Russell photographed by Reeves of Lewes

the Russell family firm with George making the shoes and selling them and his wife looking after the accounts – and in due time bearing and raising five children.

In his later years only increasing deafness prevented Albion One from seeking higher civic office. He remained a member of the Sussex Archeological Society, which he had joined in 1854, and of the Lewes Chrysanthemum Society, until his death in 1888 at his home, Priory Villa, Southover. It was from there that the funeral cortege processed to the funeral service from which the coffin was escorted by the mayor of Lewes, Alderman White, and other civic dignitaries to the old cemetery off Rotten Row for burial. To his son, Albion Two, he

TO THE

HIGH CONSTABLES

OF THE

BOROUGH OF LEWES.

In consequence of the closing of the Banks under the New Bank Act, on TUESDAY, the 26th December next, and also as the Lewes Cattle and Corn Markets will be postponed until the following day, We, the undersigned, Merchants, Tradesmen, and others, respectfully request that you will call upon the Inhabitants of the Town to close their respective business places, and set apart TUESDAY, the 26th DECEMBER, as a PUBLIC HOLIDAY.

Browne & Crosskey, Warehousemen
James Broad, Merchant
Benj. Flint and Son, Grocers and Tea Dealers
Thomas Madgwick, Grocer
E. Morris and Sons, Iron Merchants
George Martin, Grocer
Wilmshurst & Son, Fruit Merchants
Charles A. Wells, Ironmonger and Founder
Arthur H. Browning, Wine Merchant
Lowdell, Cooper and Co., Ironmongers
Dennett Huggett and Son, Butchers
George Huggett, Boot Maker
R. C. Hobden, Sewing Machine Depot
C. Coppinger, Tailor
H. Gorringe, Butcher
Thomas E. Beard, Brewer
William Page Green, Draper, &c.
Albion Russell, Boot Manufacturer
William Nurse, Hat Maker
S. and C. Mitchell, Silk Mercers
John Fuller, Draper, &c.
Gates and Bailey, Leather Cutters
Benj. Morris, Butcher
E. Monk and Sons, Brewers
W. Ayling, Draper
Harvey and Son, Brewers
Wm. Price, Grocer
Jas. Hannam, Tailor and Outfitter
Baxter and Arkcoll, Tanners
A. Elmsley, Brewer
Thomas Figg, Chemist
J. and A. Hillman, Brewers
Funnell and Hillman, Grocers, &c.

James Shaw, Grocer
Cheale and Sons, Engineers
W. P. Davey, Butcher
W. R. Stepney, Draper, &c.
Solomon Savage, Wholesale Stationer
John Harland, Baker
W. Mann, Dyer
John Chapman, Watchmaker
Joseph Andrew Lipscombe, Butcher
Charles Parsons, Mason
Parsons Bros., Timber and Slate Merchants
John Every, Iron Founder
Joseph King, General Merchant
Joseph Shelley, Miller, &c.
A. Hoadley, Grocer
Davey and Son, Sadlers, &c.
Albert Pam, Chemist
James Richards, Bookseller
T. and G. Carvill, Upholsterers
G. A. Jenner, Grocer
M. Watts, Milliner
H. Boulton Adkins, Watchmaker
Edward Adkins, Gunmaker
Henry Tucker Stapley, Stationer, &c.
Josiah Weller, Saddler and Harness Maker
C. J. Harris, House Agent
E. Bedford, Grocer
G. Humble and Son, Tea Dealers
Stevens and Shelley, Tobacconists
Henry Curtis, Chemist
Henry Mills, Draper
Chas. Simmonds, Builder
John Lutman, Watchmaker
H. Smith, Greengrocer
William Hall, Grocer

. Cuttenden, Confectioner
M. A. Rumsey, Fancy Draper
Mrs. Berry, Berlin Wool and Fancy Repository
Peter Tickner, Draper and Outfitter
Geo. Wood, Cutler
B. Thorpe, Builder
Jos. Watford, Butcher
H. Card and Son, Builders and Contractors
James Hammond, Confectioner
Thomas Manning, Grocer
J. Newington, China Warehouseman
Samuel Love, Linen Draper
Geo. W. Green, Baker and Mealman
S. Tanner, Watch and Clock Maker
S. Solomon, Watchmaker, &c., &c.
James Butland, Bookseller
E. H. W. Roswell, Chemist, &c.
J. Hardwick, Draper
J. Spencelayh, Fancy Warehouse
Thos. Hardy, Tobacconist
M. Mond, Hatter and Outfitter
John Knight, Builder
William Hammond, Upholsterer
H. Mercer, Fruiterer and Seedsman
W. E. Mannington, Grocer, &c.
W. Alderton, Baker
William Payne, Draper, &c.
G. Lindfield, Bootmaker
G. Sandals, Grocer
Arthur Kemp, Plumber, &c.
J. Rouse, Wholesale Tobacconist
John West, Grocer
J. Kenward, Fruiterer & Seedsman
Thomas James, Builder
William Banks, General News and Advertising Agent

In compliance with the above we invite the Merchants, Traders, and other Inhabitants of Lewes to adopt the suggestion of the Requisitionists and to observe

TUESDAY, THE 26TH DAY OF DECEMBER, AS A PUBLIC HOLIDAY.

Record Room, Lewes, 1st December, 1871.

WM. DUPLOCK, } High Constables
of the
THOS. BANCE, (Borough of Lewes.

GEO. P. BACON, SUSSEX ADVERTISER AND STEAM PRINTING OFFICES, LEWES.

Boxing Day was a working day in Britain until the Bank Acts of the 1870s made it, and Easter Monday, Whit Monday and the first Monday in August a holiday for some, but not all, workers.

The Russell boot and shoe factory premises on Cliffe bridge. Today the
building houses the Riverside arcade of shops.

Albion Two (1858-1930) with his family. Back row (l to r): Ernest Clifford,
Arthur Leslie, Frederick Albion. Centre (seated): Beatrice May, Albion Two,
Florence and (standing) Reginald. In foreground: Margaret Edith and
Winifred Doris.

left his three main shops at Lewes, Newhaven and East Grinstead and to his married daughter the Russell and Bromley shop in Eastbourne.

Albion Two shared his late father's entrepreneurial commercial spirit – although not his great interest in civic affairs. He was a Freemason, a member of the Lewes Cyclists' Club, and when in 1913 he moved to 144 Dyke Road, Brighton, where he lived until his death in 1930, he was an active member of the Brighton Cruising Club and later its commodore.

To take full advantage of the means of mass production he had at his disposal in the manufactory on Cliffe bridge, which was at that time employing twenty people, Albion Two established a chain of Russell shops throughout Sussex to act as retail outlets for the boots and shoes it was producing.

He was joined in the enterprise by his son, Ernest Clifford, and together they opened two shops at Brighton, one at Newhaven, one at East Grinstead, one at Seaford, and took over the Golden Boot in West Street, Horsham which had belonged since the early 1820s to their kinsmen, the Thorpe/Taylor families.

Ernest Russell added two more shops to the list – at Bognor Regis in 1927 and at Haywards Heath in 1937. However, little is known about the history of these ventures and by 1947 the firm of A Russell and Son had been sold to Ernest's sister, Elizabeth's, family – the Bromleys – and incorporated into Russell and Bromley.

This effectively brought together as one firm the two businesses which had gone their independent ways since 1888, although the joint names had been in use since Elizabeth Russell married George Frederick Bromley and inherited her father's shop in Eastbourne.

With the death in 1970 of Ernest Clifford Russell, who had only held a consultancy non-executive role in Russell and Bromley, the business link of Russells with Bromleys ended.

The Bromley family had, in fact, gained complete control in 1947. Ernest Clifford Russell had married Dorothy Whiteman but they had no children and he left three unmarried sisters in Hove. He survived two other sisters and three brothers. Arthur Leslie, 1890–1970, was a Flight Lieutenant in the Royal Flying Corps and a prisoner of war for three years during the First World War. On his return to civilian life he became traffic manager at the old Croydon aerodrome, which was then the airport for London. When Arthur Leslie retired to Waldron,

near Heathfield he set up as a chicken farmer. His wife, Octavia survived him and lived for some years at 10 Priory Crescent, Lewes, later moving to Beaminster, Dorset to live near her daughters.

Reginald, 1894–1970, emigrated to Australia in the 1920s and married Aileen ('Billie') Robjohns. They had a family which included an only son who was christened Albion after his grandfather and great grandfather. Sadly, he did not use the name and became known as 'Robin'. He was, however, the main beneficiary in the will of his aunt, Margaret Edith, the last surviving child of Albion Two's large family. Edith had inherited the estates left by her two sisters – Beatrice May who died in 1982, and Winifred Doris who died in 1983.

Ernest Clifford, 1886-1970, second son of Albion Two, was the last to bear the Russell name in the firm of Russell and Bromley.

The only other brother, Frederick Albion, 1884–1968, had suspect mental health from early manhood and was never able to establish himself very successfully in the commercial world. These were the factors that brought about the need to dispose of the A Russell and Son businesses on Ernest Clifford's retirement.

Because of the family ties between Russell and Bromley, as well as the former business liaison, it is satisfying to consider that the Bromley great grandchildren of Albion One Russell, Peter and Roger, are now the heads of the company.

8

TIME AND THE BROMLEYS

IT was as a clockmaker that Michael Bromley, born 1748, started in business at Maresfield. He may have moved on to East Grinstead, because a son, John, was born there in 1778 or 1779. By 1804 Michael was established as a clockmaker and silversmith in Horsham and spent the rest of his life in that town.

John followed into his father's business. In the Horsham museum there are three clocks with painted dials and three verge watches engraved 'John Bromley'. Other examples of his work are in private hands and one of his descendants, Michael Cornish Bromley, possesses a clock marked 'Bromley, Horsham'

On the left of the main entrance to Horsham parish churchyard from the Causeway is the gravestone of John's wife, Ann Godson, who died on December 6 1840, aged sixty. On it is 'also of John Bromley who died May 26 1854'.

John's marriage to Ann produced at least four children, Ann, born in 1809; Michael, born 1812; John Roger, born 1814; and Susan, born 1816. The eldest, Michael, joined his father's firm in West Street and is listed in trade and town directories for Horsham in 1830 as 'John Bromley, trading as M Bromley'. Henry Burstow, in his reminiscences, records that in 1837 'thieves broke into Michael Bromley's shop and stole £400 of goods'.

After his father's death the second son, John Roger, took himself off to Hastings and *Melville's Directory* lists him with a tea and Italian warehouse business at 9 George Street in the Old Town. He became an Alderman of the Borough of Hastings during the mayoralty of George Archibald Thorpe, whose own shoemaking business was at 22 George Street.

For the second time in the Bromley story a son eschewed the established family business. John Roger's son, George Frederick Bromley, went in 1873 as an apprentice to Albion Russell, the shoemaker son of John-Clifford Russell of Chiddingly, at 187-188 High Street, Lewes.

He courted and married his employer's eldest daughter, Elizabeth Jane, on November 2 1874 and on their return from honeymoon in West Norwood, Croydon, they were given the management of Albion Russell's shop at 47 Seaside Road, Eastbourne. At first they lived over the shop but later moved to 7 Upperton Gardens and then to Bineham in St Leonard's Road, a house since demolished to make way for the extension of the railway station complex.

The Eastbourne shop, which was near the junction with Bourne Street, continued as A Russell and Co for a time but by 1878 was listed in the town directory as Russell and Bromley – the first time that the joint names appeared on a fascia.

Other premises were found on the corner of Terminus Road and Gildredge Road, which had been laid out as a shopping area some thirty years previously.

Number 114 Terminus Road was formerly

7 Upperton Gardens, Eastbourne in the 1980s.

Cripps, a shoemaker, and its front entrance, when it was refitted around 1932, had ceramic footprints placed in the lobby entrance. In 1890 Number 116B was leased with the recently introduced wonder of the telephone adding status to the addresses, *viz.* telephone number 40 for 116B and 40B for 47 Seaside Road.

By 1890 the couple had four sons and a daughter. The eldest, Frederick Russell Bromley, 1876–1943, gained practical experience of the manufacturing side of the shoemaking business at an early age under his uncle Albion Two, then head of the Russell business at Lewes. He progressed rapidly and by the age of eighteen he was able to take charge of the Eastbourne shops which was all to the good as his father had suffered a fall in the shop some years previously and his health was deteriorating. In 1897 he died, at the age of forty five.

There is no doubt that Frederick Russell Bromley was the entrepreneur who took the company into the twentieth century. He saw selling footwear rather than making shoes as the way to further fortune, and he built on the solid reputation of the Russells as bespoke shoemakers.

With his mother's help he took over a small bootmaker's shop in Tonbridge, Kent, which he ran with the previous owner under the names of Gale and Bromley. Another shop

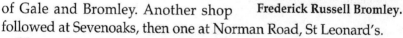

Frederick Russell Bromley.

followed at Sevenoaks, then one at Norman Road, St Leonard's.

He nearly over-reached himself when he acquired premises at 21 Widmore Road, Bromley, Kent, from the Gale family and in 1901 had to appeal to his uncle, Albion, to help him out. However, dogged persistence prevailed and by 1920 he had a second shop in Bromley – in purpose-built premises at 140 High Street – trading under the name of A Russell. He had asked his uncle Albion for permission to use his name in this new venture.

By 1909 his mother had relinquished control of the business and the document of transfer was witnessed by a Russell cousin, Clifford (John Clifford) then of Sevenoaks, Kent.

By 1910 Frederick Russell Bromley had five shops – four of them owned by his uncle, Albion Two. He married Hilda Underwood, who came from Taunton, and she became an important member of the firm. In 1923 when Russell and Bromley became a limited company, she was one of the first two directors. Mrs. Hilda Bromley gave forty years' service to the business, carrying on almost unaided during the First World War.

Another member of the family, Frederick Russell's sister Edith Gertrude (Aunt Bess), was hosiery buyer for the company for most of her working life. She did not marry and lived with her mother in the family home in the Bromley area.

The year 1933 brought the first shop-within-a-shop in the United Kingdom – a branch of Jaeger within the Torquay premises. This was followed by Ricemans of Canterbury, now Fenwicks, where Russell and Bromley still operate. In 1939 a new shop in Eastbourne replaced the two smaller ones in Terminus Road. It was demolished when the town was heavily bombed in 1943 and was rebuilt after the war on the same site.

A 1931 bill for shoe repairs for a member of staff.

There were sixteen shops in the company by the time Frederick Russell retired in 1935. He died in 1943, aged sixty seven. His two sons, Frederick Keith (Toby), born 1912, and Michael Cornish, born 1914, took control. Both young men served in the Armed Forces during the Second World War and the management of Russell and Bromley was left with two colleagues, Mr Menpes and Mr Huard, and Miss Edith and Mrs Hilda Bromley.

The coming of peace brought upheaval, change and achievement, and the firm's expansion from this time owes much to the vision and drive of its managing director, Michael Bromley.

In 1947 Russell and Bromley opened a store in New Bond Street, London and the following year took over Lederer, an Austrian firm famous for handbags. Its branch in Knightsbridge gave Russell and Bromley its second prime address in the capital. In the following years seven new shops were opened in Central London and two existing shops enlarged – at Knightsbridge and Chelsea. In 1959 the need for new headquarters to replace those in Widmore Road, Bromley resulted in the purchase of the site of an old sawmill in Farwig Lane. It was large enough to cater for extensions and in 1987 a second warehouse was constructed on the site.

Keith retired as chairman in 1967 and his brother, Michael, was appointed in his place. Further changes were to take place under the new chairman/managing director's control. His two sons, Peter and Roger, were appointed to the Board and in 1968 the Bond Street premises were reconstructed and in the following years big branches established. In 1970 Keith decided to sever his connections with Russell and Bromley and devote himself to his other interests, which included farming in Scotland, where he bred award-winning Aberdeen Angus cattle. He was a keen naturalist and built an all metal yacht in which he sailed to the Antarctic to study the penguins. He later established a 'tropical rain forest experience' at Wyld Court, near Newbury in Berkshire. It is now run by the World Land Trust as an Educational and Visitors' Centre. His two sons were not anxious to follow in the family firm but Michael's children chose to do so.

In 1973 Peter and Roger were made joint managing directors, with their father, Michael, remaining as chairman.

Further shops were opened in Marble Arch, Oxford Street and Greater London. At Brent Cross, where the company had been for ten years, a second 'children's only' shop appeared in 1986. Branches were opened at Bath and Exeter and the famous Russell and Bromley fascia went up over premises in Princes Street, Edinburgh and at Harrogate, Leeds, Southport and Chester. Premises were acquired in the Metro-Centre, Gateshead, the largest shopping complex in Europe – all big powerful shops in powerful centres.

This vigorous expansion of major shops in most of the important

Managing director Roger Bromley, the then chairman Michael Bromley, current chairman Peter Bromley, and John England Crowther, personnel director, at Russell and Bromley's centenary celebrations at the Grosvenor House Hotel on May 7 1979.

English towns and Scotland's capital, led to the closure of about a third of the shops in the smaller centres, an operation which was completed in 1970/1.

In 1997 there was a return to full family ownership when the shoe company, Bally, sold back to Russell and Bromley the interest which it had purchased in 1963. There are now forty-two retail outlets in the chain, with sales well in excess of £50 millions annually. About 1,000 people make up the workforce of which some 900 are in the retail shops. Many of them are second generation employees.

Peter is currently chairman and joint managing director with his brother, Roger. Their sister, Mrs Anthony Howeson, (Nicola), formerly actively involved in the company, is a shareholder, along with, directly or indirectly, all the grandchildren of Michael and Molly Bromley, who now live in retirement in Surrey. It has given the family great pleasure that Peter's son, Andrew Michael Bromley, born in 1968, has recently joined the family concern as, it is expected, his brother Stuart Peter, born 1971, will do in the near future.

APPENDIX I

Russell – the Chiddingly branch

IN the 1770s Robert, an agricultural labourer, and his wife, Ann, lived in Chiddingly. No positive marriage record has been found to date but they had twelve children, all baptised in Chiddingly church.
They were:

Robert, b1772.
Elizabeth, 1774–1777.
Mary, 1775–1857. Mother of John-Clifford Russell.
Martha, b1777.   Became Mrs Parsons.
Alice, b1780.   Became Mrs Turner?
Hannah, b1781.   Became Mrs Akehurst.
William, b1784.   Married Hannah —? and had six children.
Susan, b1786.   Known as Ayhorn in adult life.
Edward, b1788.
John, b1791 – the same year as his uncle, John-Clifford Russell.
Sarah, b1793.
Miller, 1795–1876

On October 3 1792 the parents were removed to Hellingly parish by the Overseers of the Poor but two of their twelve children remained in Chiddingly. Mary was 'put out' to Mr Joseph Willard from 1787 to 1788 and again in March 1789. Martha went to Mr Sam Holman from 1787 to 1788 and to Mr Richard White from 1789 to 1790.

GEORGE CLIFFORD RUSSELL, eldest son of John-Clifford Russell, Cordwainer of Chiddingly, was married twice. His first wife was Jane Taylor, a widow.

Issue:

John Norman Russell, 1845–1909
Lydia Jane Russell, 1849-1915

His second marriage was to Johanna Anable on 11 December 1851.

Issue:

Joseph Clifford 1852-1934
Harriett 1854-1873
Elizabeth Ann b1857. Became Mrs Thomas Simmonds of Lewes.

John Norman, a bootmaker, married Sarah Jane Coote in 1873. He died on 5 April 1909 at 24 Rushams Road, Horsham and was buried in Hills Road cemetery. His wife died on 28 July 1941 at the home of her son George Ernest at Kirby Cross, Frinton-on-Sea, Essex.

Their issue:

NORMAN CLIFFORD, b1875 at Uckfield.
GEORGE ERNEST, b1876 at Uckfield. Died 1959.
ELIZABETH MAUD, b1878 at Uckfield.
PERCY HAROLD, b1880 at Uckfield.
CHARLES HENRY, b1882 at Hastings.
EDITH ANNIE, b1884 at Horsham.
ALBION (III), b1887 at Pulborough.
WILLIAM (III), b1889 at Pulborough.

NORMAN CLIFFORD married Florence Edmunds. He died of tuberculosis at Nunhead, London in 1901, aged 26. Their son, also a Norman, b1898, lost both parents as a baby – his mother and sister died of typhoid. He was brought up by his grandparents and killed, aged 18, in the last year of the First World War.

GEORGE ERNEST first married Mary Freeston in 1905. Their son died of diphtheria. By his second wife, Emily Barlow, who he married in 1910, he had three children – Victor, b1910; Rita, b1911; and Peter, b1921. George Ernest had a distinguished career in the Metropolitan Police, in which he served for twenty five years, retiring in 1924. For the last fourteen years he was in charge of the photographic section of the Public Carriage Office at Scotland Yard and was credited with having taken 265,000 photographs using four tons of plates. Before being transferred to the Yard, Sergeant Russell was commended by the Commissioner on eight occasions. He also received the Royal Humane Society medal and certificate for saving a woman from drowning, almost at the cost of his own life. He took up printing when he retired to Kirby Cross, Frinton, Essex and was joined in the business by his son Victor.

ELIZABETH MAUD did not marry. She became a ladies' maid at St Albans.

PERCY HAROLD married and lived at Alton, Hampshire. The couple had a son named John Clifford Russell (iii).

CHARLES HENRY died of tuberculosis in 1907.

EDITH ANNIE lived at 30 Spencer Road, Horsham with her parents. She remained a spinster.

ALBION (III) had a military career, serving in the 1st Lifeguards. He married Edith Murphy and the couple lived at Storrington, West Sussex.

WILLIAM (III) spent his working life in the London Fire Brigade and lived at Dulwich. He married Lilian Jacobs, 1888-1978, and they had two daughters – Joy Elizabeth, b5 May1929, who married Kenneth Holdsworth of Yorkshire, 1927-1990, (no issue) and Jeanne Eileen, b 24 June 1924. She married Victor Colinridge and died in October 1995 without issue.

Lydia Jane (i) was born on 2 September 1849 in Uckfield. Her mother, the writer of the diary of that year, died in January 1850 and she was reared at home by her father and a housekeeper until he remarried in 1851.

Lydia married a draper's assistant, Frederic Smith, 1850-1894, at Holy Cross church, Uckfield on 10 June 1879. They lived firstly at Newick and then moved to a house in Castle Hill, Rotherfield where he became a grocer's manager, and finally at Longcroft, Rotherfield. Both are buried in St Denys churchyard at Rotherfield.

Issue:

GEORGE FREDERICK, b23 June 1880 at Newick. Died at Portsmouth.

HARRY NORMAN, b Rotherfield 5 October 1881. Died 1915.
CLIFFORD RUSSELL, b Rotherfield 5 April 1883. Died 1952.
ALICE HARRIETT, b Rotherfield 17 September 1884. Died 1942.
LYDIA JANE (II), b Rotherfield 13 September 1886.
EDITH MAY, b Rotherfield 1888. Died 1889.
ALBION PERCY, b Rotherfield 16 January 1890. Died 1977.
WILLIAM GLADSTONE, b Rotherfield 20 September 1891. Died 1961.
ELIZABETH MAUD, b Rotherfield 2 June 1894. Died 1967.

GEORGE FREDERICK. Gunner No. 57677 in the Royal Field Artillery from 1915 to 1918 . Married and lived in Portsmouth.

HARRY NORMAN. Corporal in 5th Battalion, Royal Sussex Regiment. He died of disease on active service in 1915 and his name is on Roll of Honour in St Denys church, Rotherfield.

CLIFFORD RUSSELL, known as 'Jack', lived in Rotherfield all his life. He was a gardener and general labourer. He married Alice Jane Vans and they had four children:

Jack Frederick, 1915-1993, who married Vivian Moore and had three children – Robert, b1948; Janice, b1949; and Carol, b1958.
Vera Phyllis Russell, 1917-1988. No issue.
Albert Charles Henry, 1924-1995, married Rita Baldock and had two daughters – Josephine and Sally
Doris Ruby May, 1929-1996, married Frank Atkinson. No issue.

ALICE HARRIETT was killed in a street accident in the blackout in Brighton in 1942. She had three children who each bore the surname Smith:

Alice (Babs), 1908-1988, married Bert Harman. They had three sons, Dennis, Kenneth and Michael. The latter was mayor of Newhaven in 1987.
Alfred Clifford (Busty), 1917-1995, married Valentine May King, b14 February 1920, in 1939. They had a son, Norman, b1952.
Frederick Gladstone New, 1915-1995, married Betty Arrow. They had a daughter, Betty-Ann.

WILLIAM GLADSTONE SMITH married Margaret Jones in 1925. They had a daughter, Jean, b1929. She married Len Watson in 1952 and they had two children, Timothy Robert (Tom), b1956 and Nicholas David, b1958. The marriage ended in divorce.

ELIZABETH MAUD SMITH, 1894-1967, married Arthur Grace. No issue.

LYDIA JANE (II) married Tom Chuter. They had one son, Reginald, and lived at Five Ashes, near Heathfield.

EDITH MAY died as a baby in 1889. A family legend says that her mother 'saw an angel' the night before the child died.

ALBION PERCY was given the name Albion (meaning England) after his mother's cousin, Albion Russell. He was put to sea by the Lady of the Manor of Rotherfield, Miss Catherine Pullein, who took an interest in the young lad and left him a small legacy in her will. Albion spent twenty three years in the Royal and Merchant Navies. During the 1914–18 war he was valet to Rear-Admiral Sir Henry Ralph Crooke on HMS *Caroline*, a light cruiser engaged at the Battle of Jutland. Fifty years later, Albion was a guest aboard the old ship, now permanently moored as a training vessel in Belfast Dry Dock, at a dinner attended by the Duke of Edinburgh to mark the anniversary. He was one of the only three remaining veteran members of the ship's company from that engagement who were present. After the war, he joined the Merchant Navy as a steward and visited most of the major ports of the world.

He married Violet Irene Rosa Kirk, b15 April 1898, on 1 October 1921 at St Catherine's church, Hatcham, London and the couple made their home at 66, Malpas Road, Brockley, SE4. The bride was the only child of Florence Louise, neé Mayo, and Joseph (Groves) Kirk, an artist and engraver of Bristol. In 1934, the family – by then they had two daughters – left London for Minstead in the New Forest where Albion Percy Smith became steward of the village community centre. Violet, who had had poor health all her life, brought on by rheumatic fever as a child, rallied in the country air for some years and died at Lyndhurst Cottage Hospital on 8 January 1951 and was cremated at Stoneham near Southampton.

On the death of his employer, Mr Daniel Hanbury, in 1951 Albion returned to sea, signing on for voyages to Australia in the *Esperence Bay*. In letters home he declared the crew were 'cowboys' and could not endure the sloppy conditions and attitude of the 'so called seamen'. Back in England he lived firstly with his eldest daughter, José, at Swan Green, Lyndhurst and then with his younger daughter, Olive, at 67 Springfield Avenue, Merton Park before leasing a lonely cottage at the Mill House, Weston-by-Welland, Northants, where he lived very contentedly for several years.

He was persuaded to return south with advancing years, when an opportunity occurred for him to become a resident in warden-controlled flats at the Royal Alfred Seamen's Society homes at Banstead, Surrey. He was staying temporarily with Olive in Merton Park when he died on 25 April 1977. The funeral took place at Woodmansterne Church followed by cremation at Croydon.

Issue:
Iris Josephine, b4 July 1922 at Brockley, London.
Olive Gwendoline, b19 October 1924 at Brockley, London.

Iris Josephine (José) married twice, first, on her twenty first birthday in 1943 at Minstead church in the New Forest, to Kenneth Royston Davis of Lancaster, b27 February 1919, a wartime soldier in the Royal Armoured Corps. He died at Cordwainer's, Chiddingly on 19 July 1988 of cancer and his ashes are buried in Chiddingly churchyard. The couple had three children:

Kelvin John, b28 May 1945 at Lancaster.
Nigel Bruce, b11 December 1946 at Lyndhurst, Hampshire.
Helen Josephine, b5 September 1949, also at Lyndhurst.

Kelvin married Ann Cheshire of Sundridge, Bromley, Kent on 19 February 1966. The marriage ended in divorce in 1973. He is now partnered by Valerie Patricia Tolliday and lives at Shooters Hill, London SE 18.

Issue:
Jacqueline Ann, b27 December 1966.
Adrian Kelvin, b19 June 1971.

Nigel married Judy Viner at St Lawrence church, Morden, Surrey on 28 April 1973. The family live at Claygate, Surrey.

Issue:
Laura Viner, b14 February 1982.
Patrick Charles, b26 April 1985.
Isabel Clare, b11 December 1987.

Iris Josephine secondly married Edward Samuel Loosemore, b27 August 1912, of Eastbourne, on 31 March 1990 at Chiddingly parish church.

Olive Gwendoline married a headmaster, Charles William Thornton, b1913 of Hilgay in Norfolk, at All Saints Church, Minstead, Hampshire on 26 October 1946. He died at his home at Old Cottage, Warnham, Horsham on 8 March 1983.

Issue:

Jane, b28 August 1947. She died two weeks later at Farnham, Surrey.
Janice, b12 April 1949 at Farnborough, Kent. She is a college tutor and lives at Stoke Newington.
Elizabeth, b26 January 1951, also at Farnborough. She married Dottorio Marco Valentine, a veterinary surgeon of Arezzo, Italy at Horsham on 27 August 1981. They have a daughter, Jessica, b8 May 1982, and live at Sellia Marina, Catanzaro, Calabria.

Joseph Clifford, bootmaker, married Ann —? 1851–1933.

Issue:
Annie Violet, married Patrick (Martin?)
Ethel Daisy, married Roger (Fitch?)

JULIUS RUSSELL, 1819–1898, the second son and fourth child of John-Clifford Russell of Chiddingly and his wife, Jane, set up as a tea and general grocer at 20 West Street, the main shopping street of Horsham, in 1848. A commercial directory of 1907–8 gives 20 West Street and the Bishopric as his two addresses. His uncle, John Thorpe, (his mother's brother) was trading in West Street as a 'draper, mercer and shoemaker' in 1830, according to the *Recollections of Henry Burstow*, published in 1911. Julius may have initially joined his

Julius Russell.
Photo by Edward Reeves

uncle when the business was described as that of a draper/undertaker. He married Mary Smart, daughter of William and Charlotte Smart of Horsham. Mary died October 24 1876, aged 59, and is buried in her parents' grave.

Issue:

Mary J, b1848? Spinster?

Annie. Wife of Frederick Bennett?

William Smart b1849. Died July 15 1930.

John Clifford (ii), b1850? Died 1934 or 1935

Charlotte

Julius made a will dated June 5 1886. He died on July 16 1898 and was buried in Horsham cemetery on July 21. Probate was granted at Chichester in August – effects £2,112. The trustees were his son-in-law, Frederick Bennett, who was married to either Mary J or Annie, and his eldest son William Smart. The business was left on lease to his sons and continued under the name of W S Russell and Son, John Clifford (ii) having by this time set up a separate business in Sevenoaks.

William Smart was given his mother's surname as a second name. He worked with his father in the tea and general store in West Street and also became an accomplished watercolour artist. His series of eight postcards of Horsham scenes were printed by the art publisher, Salmon of Sevenoaks, in the 1920s and are much sort after by collectors today. The portrait he is believed to have painted of his father, Julius, has been lost. He features in the art directory, Hidden Talents, by art historian Jeremy Wood and was the subject of an article in Sussex Life in April 1977.

William Smart is recorded as living at Vine Cottage, 13 Bishopric from 1917 to 1918 and later at 3 Padwick Cottages, Worthing Road, Horsham. He married: 1) Caroline, who died in 1905, aged 54, and is buried in the family grave in Denne Road cemetery, and 2) Annie Mary Gilbard (or Gilburd) in 1909. She was formerly his housekeeper and was an alcoholic.

To get money for drink she took her husband's paintings to the butcher, Mr Hosken, and was given meat in exchange. In this way

William Smart Russell's painting of West Street, Horsham. One of a series of eight postcards published by Salmon of Sevenoaks.

the butcher built up a fine collection of William Smart Russell's watercolours.

Issue, by his first wife:

RALPH WILLIAM. Baptised June 11 1883. Died April 14 1918. He worked with his father in the grocers shop. Enlisted at Chichester in World War I and died of trench fever at Devonport, having served in the 13th Battalion of the Royal Sussex Regiment, Lowther's Lambs. His name is inscribed on Horsham war memorial. An official War Graves Commission tombstone was erected on the family grave plot in Denne Road cemetery.

Ralph married Ethel Attwater. She died on April 2 1966, aged 78. Her family were in business in the town from 1883 as plumbers and painters at 16 Market Square. *No issue.*

William Smart and his first wife, Caroline, may have had a second child. There is an inscription on the kerb of the family grave to 'Irene, died May 17 1899 '.

John Clifford (ii) was born at Horsham and later lived at nearby Broadbridge Heath. He worked with his father in the grocery business and about 1890 went to Sevenoaks, Kent, and established a business there which was considered to be the Fortnum and Mason of the town.

He married Emma Streater, whose parents were blacksmiths at Billingshurst in West Sussex. Emma became an alcoholic and the business failed. However, it was said that by sheer will-power she cured herself and the couple attempted a new life. He trained as a market gardener, and moved to Devon to an old thatched house called Gardiners Hall at Bradford-on-Tone. This was destroyed by fire and they moved to Weare Gifford. Their son, Ernest Clifford (John), carried on a market garden on the site of the old house.

Issue:

HILDA RUTH, 1884/5–1959. She became a governess in Argentina and married a New Zealand rancher, Hugh Nairn. Their son, John (1922?–1962) became a rancher in the Argentine. They also had a daughter, Adela.

EVELYN. Married Fred Wenban-Smith, who later established a builder's merchant company in Worthing, and whose family came from the Ticehurst/Wadhurst area of Sussex where there is still a house called Wenbans. The couple had four children – three daughters, Helen, Margaret and Barbara, and a son, William (Bill) who was born on June 8 1908 and had a most distinguished career.

Bill Wenban-Smith was in the Colonial Administrative Service from 1931 to 1961 and was Speaker of the Legislature of Nyasaland 1961–3, and in the Diplomatic Service at Kuala Lumpur 1964–9. He became a Commander of the Order of the British Empire (CBE) in 1957 and and a Commander of the Order of St Michael and St George (CMG) in 1960.

His book *Walks in the New Forest*, was published in 1975. He married Ruth Orme McElderry and they had five children, three sons and two daughters. In retirement they lived at Milford-on-Sea, Hampshire. One son, William Nigel, born 1936, followed his father into the

Diplomatic Service and became Deputy High Commissioner at Ottowa in 1986.

ERNEST CLIFFORD (i) (John) 1887–1977, the third child of John Clifford (ii) and Emma, married three times – to Mary White of Minehead in 1914; to Gladys Cousens of Taunton in 1933; and to Muriel (Murry) Walden of Tiverton in 1960 (on January 19, her husband's birthday). He had two daughters by his second wife, Jill, born in 1935 and Susan in 1937.

CHARLOTTE. Dates not known. Married Robert Crowhurst, a Brighton tailor, and lived at 57, Beaconsfield Villas. Her aunt by marriage, Sarah Jane Russell, wife of Albion (i), died at her home in 1905.

> ## COUSINS – BY COINCIDENCE.
>
> Ernest Clifford (i) held shares in ICI and received a proxy form from the company which should have gone to Ernest Clifford Russell (ii) of Lewes. Both men were born in the same year, 1887, and they found that they were cousins.

AUTHOR'S NOTE: It was from Murry Russell, whom I contacted through Bill Wenban-Smith, that I obtained details of Julius Russell and his descendants.

ALBION RUSSELL (i) 1821–1888, third son and fifth child of John-Clifford Russell, Cordwainer of Chiddingly, married Sarah Jane, née Willard, in Lewes in 1849.

Issue:

Elizabeth Jane, born March 20 1850, died 1937. She married George Frederick Bromley on November 2 1874 at St John's Church, Lewes.

Sarah Anne, born February 22 1852, died 1901. She married George Peter Broad, tallow manufacturer, in 1875 and they had eleven children.

Ellen Willard, born February 4 1854, died March 1858

Frederick George, born March 14 1856, died 1858.

Albion (ii), born January 10 1858, died April 8 1930.

Fanny Cordelia, born December 18 1859, died 1860.

Edith, born January 31 1861, died July 13 1934.

Emily Maria, born June 19 1863, died November 28 1958.

Albion Russell (ii) married twice, first to Harriett Martin, 1858–1905, daughter of Frederick and Margaret Martin of 38, Cliffe, Lewes. She died at the family home, Saxthorpe, The Wallands, Lewes, aged 46 and was buried in St Michael's cemetery.

Issue:

FLORENCE ALICE, 1881–1953. Spinster.
HARRIETT, 1883–1892. Spinster. Known as "Tottie'.
FREDERICK ALBION, 1884–1968. Nigerian State Railway employee.
ERNEST CLIFFORD, 1886–1970.
BEATRICE MAY, 1888–1982.
ARTHUR LESLIE, 1890–1970.
REGINALD, 1894–1970.
WINIFRED DORIS, 1898–1983.
MARGARET EDITH, 1902–1988.

Albion Russell (ii)'s second marriage was to Alice Sawyer who became his housekeeper on the death of Harriett. They had no children.

ARTHUR LESLIE RUSSELL married Octavia Bullen-Lund, b1903.

Issue:

Vivian Harriett, b1923, married Peter Bell and they have five children, Elizabeth, John, Mary, Christine and Michael.
Pauline Leslie, b1927, married David Frazer Brown. They have two children, Virginia Mary and Nicholas.

REGINALD RUSSELL emigrated to Australia where he married Aileen Maude Robjohns, b1915. He served in the Australian Imperial Force in the First World War and later became a fruit farmer in Adelaide.

Issue:

1) *Robin Albion Russell,* b1947. He married Christina Margaret Davey and they have two sons, David Andrew Russell, b1969 and Paul Albion Russell, b1972. The marriage ended in divorce. He has formed a second partnership with Colleen Patricia Windle, b1957.
2) *Helen Mary Russell,* b1948. She married Ha Duong, b1946. They have three children, Robin, b1971; Emma, b1974; and Thomas, b1976.
3) *Elise Joy,* b1949. She has one child, Sok Puthea Russell, b1974.

AUTHOR'S NOTE: I had a small case of family memorabilia and documents which had been given to me by a Russell relative to look after. I received a telephone call from Robin Albion Russell of Canberra, to say that he was in Lewes and would like to meet me. He called with Colleen Windle, his partner, on the June 20 1996 and I was able to hand over the precious documents which Robin was happy to receive and these have formed a basis for his own researches.

JANE RUSSELL (II) was the sixth child of John-Clifford Russell of Chiddingly. She was born on 4 July (the same birthdate as José Loosemore) 1824 and after her father's death in 1850 she continued to live at home with her mother. On 26 July 1852, at Chiddingly church, she married John Andrews, a draper and grocer of Storrington.

He was the son of James Andrews, a sawyer of Storrington. James was said to have been left a property named Perrotts in Storrington in 1792. John Andrews was a tenant of Colonel Wyndham of 'a cottage and two gardens' at Hurston, about two fields away from Perrots. In 1852, John bought his shop in West Street, Storrington from George Greenfield and sold it to his apprentice, James Greenfield, in 1864. The family moved to Lewes in 1865. John was at one time manager for Browne and Crosskey, drapers in Cliffe High Street and he later became proprietor of a business in Slough, Bucks where his son James, in business with him, became president of the Slough Chamber of Commerce. Jane Andrews' portion of his inheritance from her father, J-C Russell, of £210 was paid and a receipt for it signed by her husband, John.

Details from the parish register of baptisms at Storrington were sent to me by local historian, Mrs Joan Ham. The entries are:

1853 July 3 Elizabeth, daughter of John and J Andrews; 1855 April 1 Anne daughter of John and J Andrews; 1856 August 3 Jane daughter of John and J Andrews; 1858 February 7 James son of John and J Andrews; 1859 August 7 Emily daughter of John and J Andrews; 1861 April 4 John Clifford (iv) son of John and J Andrews; 1863 February 1 Fanny daughter of John and J Andrews; 1864 September 4 Charles son of John and J Andrews.

John Clifford (iv) Andrews only lived for nine days. Elizabeth Andrews died, aged nine, in 1863. Both are buried in Storrington.

James Andrews, 1858–c1940, was still going strong, and was still a bachelor, at the age of eighty. A long account of his life and achievements appeared in the *Sussex Express* together with a photograph of him with a penny farthing bicycle on which he rode from Lewes to Hailsham and back in 1 hour 40 minutes. He spent his working life in the drapery trade, retiring in 1920 to Eastbourne but returned to end his days at Houndean, Houndean Rise, Lewes.

APPENDIX II

Dates and details of associated families.

BROAD

THE Broads had been tallow chandlers since Peter Broad, 1792–1867, set up in High Street, Rye (See *Melville's Directory* of 1858) and was at one time mayor of that Ancient Town. He was the father of James and grandfather of George Peter.

When the family joined with Russells they were candlemakers in Lewes and owned the candle factory in Market Lane which was built about 1820 and closed in 1908. Other members of the family later went into brewing and education.

Sarah Ann Russell 1852–1937, the sister of Elizabeth Jane Russell who became Mrs George Frederick Bromley, married **George Peter Broad,** b1852, in 1875. They had eleven children. He was the son of James Broad, 1824–1900, a tallow manufacturer of 4, Market Place, Lewes. The family home was Coombe House, Malling Street, Lewes. James' wife was Frances, 1821–1911, daughter of a shoemaker, George F Cosstick.

Descendants of George Peter Broad and Sarah Ann (Russell)

FRIENDS ARE NEIGHBOURS

WHEN Richard Philip Russell was teaching at King Edward's School, Godalming, a colleague, Jocelyn Bailey, showed him a photograph of the cottage at Chiddingly and told him that her brother, Hugh, and his wife Martine, lived in the end of terrace cottage, now Yew Tree House.

SOME members of this extended family have corresponded with the author over the years. Their details are:

JAMES MONTAGUE BROAD, brewer, married Lilo Kenyon. They had two daughters, Nancy, and Joan who married Arthur Fowler, a captain in the Merchant Navy. They live at The Grange, Bratoft, Skegness and have a son, John.

PHILIP RUSSELL BROAD, also a brewer, married Maude Lovelace Streatfield. They had two sons, John Russell, a brewer of Northampton and Richard Philip, a schoolmaster.

EVELYN BROAD, b1885, married William Cowderoy. Their daughter, Evelyn Sarah, b31 October 1922, married Keith Arthur Moore. One of their four daughters, Jacqueline, married Ernest Thomas. They have two children, Holly and Justin.

AUTHOR'S NOTE: Jacqueline got into touch with me through writing to Russell and Bromley inquiring about her possible connection with them

BROOK

TO the daughters of her cousin Albion (ii), Lewes bookseller and stationer **Frances Burchett Brook,** b1841, was Great Aunt Frances. Her mother was Ann Willard, sister of cordwainer Richard Willard, and she had married Thomas Spring Francis

Frances Brook died at her home Morley House, High Street, Lewes in 1925. She was the widow of stationmaster, James Brook and was buried in the grave of her mother, Ann, and her brother, Richard Francis, 1838–1858. A portrait of her, artist unknown, is extant.

THE NAME IS THE SAME

An old house called Burchetts at Whitesmith, Chiddingly, was the home of Joseph Willard and his wife Ann, neé Pagden, to whom Mary Russell, mother of John-Clifford was 'put out' between 1787–1789.
Mrs Willard died in childbirth on January 14 1792. She was forty three.

POCOCK

John Pocock, b1765, was married to Jane Norman, 1781–1861, whose sister, Martha, was the mother of Jane Russell, first wife of George Clifford Russell of Uckfield. When she died in 1850 her coffin was placed in his tomb. (See chapter 1).

He lived in Brighton and was variously, often simultaneously, a licensed victualler, maltster, coal merchant, sawyer and property owner. His business addresses included the Running Horse, formerly known as the Hen and Chickens at 14, King Street; the Bedford Brewery in Sillwood Street; the Royal Yacht, Sussex Street; and premises at 10, Montpelier Road; in Middle Street; at 13 and 14 Regent Street; in Black Lion Street; and Ivory Place. It was at this last address that his niece, Jane, lived with her first husband, George Taylor, before his death on September 9 1837. John Pocock was clerk to the Chapel Royal from 1795–1808 and clerk to the parish church of St Nicholas from 1808 until his death on June 15 1846. His will was proved in the Archdeaconry of Lewes on August 3 1846.

On November 8 1827, a special rate of ninepence in the pound was levied to pay off the arrears of debt of £326 16s 8d, incurred by the vestry. Some of this money was owed to John Pocock, whose salary as clerk had not been paid regularly for twelve years.

Issue:

Thomas, married Eliza and they may have had a child named Esther Fanny.
Robert Griffiths, died 30 June 1846, aged 17.
Charles, died 1834, aged 29.
Mary
Emily
Elizabeth
Sarah, wife of Henry Smith
A grandson: JOHN LEE POCOCK

THORPE

This particular family came from Hedgecourt, Horne, Surrey in the early 1600s, by progression through descendants to Sussex via Ifield, Buxted, Maresfiel, and Duddleswell where Richard Thorpe lived from 1670 to 1741. His son, Benjamin, 1707–1781, married Ann Sansum in 1731 at Hastings by licence. Of this large family William, 1747–1819, became a cordwainer and was himself the head of an extensive family. He bought four acres of land from David Guy of the Place Farm and was believed to have built his two cottages in The Street, Chiddingly about 1870. He was married twice, first to Mary Funnell by banns on November 20 1772 at Chiddingly Church and secondly to Ann Barrow on January 3 1784 at Chiddingly. She died in 1806 and was buried at Chiddingly.

By his first marriage there were six children:

Mary, b1773. Married Richard Davis of Wilmington, Sussex.

Hannah, b1774. Married John Goldsmith, a shoemaker of Heathfield.

Elizabeth, b1775. Married John Langford in 1795, but had illegitimate son, William Thorpe, b1793.

William (ii) b1776. Cordwainer of Horsebridge and Hellingly.

John (i) b1779. Cordwainer of Horsham.

Jane (i) b1781. Wife of John-Clifford Russell of Chiddingly.

By his second marriage there were eight children:

Thomas, b1785. Draper of Rye, Kent. Married Harriett—?

Ann, b1787. Married Thomas Smith, a mason of Brighton.

Richard, b11 May 1789. Cordwainer of Ashford, Kent. He had a son called William.

Sarah, b5 March 1791.

Benjamin, 1793–1876. Draper of Hythe and Ashford.

Phillis, b1796.

George, b1797. Cordwainer of Battle, East Sussex

Sophia, b28 June 1800. Married an Ashford, Kent auctioneer called Bailey.

WILLARD

CORDWAINER Richard Willard, b1780, had a business at 175 High Street, Lewes. He married Sarah – who died in 1827, aged 43. Their tombstone is in the closed churchyard of St Michael's, Lewes.

Richard Willard

In 1839 'Richard Willard of Lewes, Cordwainer' bought a piece of land together with the poorhouse of St John sub Castro and other buildings 'lying upon the west side of the mound under the Castle' for £190 and converted them to cottages. The site of Castle Precincts House, built by John Shelley in 1815, was formerly part of the poorhouse grounds.

An oil painting of Richard Willard, artist unknown, is now at the headquarters of Russell and Bromley at Farwig Lane, Bromley, as is an oil portrait of John-Clifford Russell. Elizabeth Russell, the grand daughter of both these men, became co-founder of the firm with her husband, George Frederick Bromley.

There is a similar portrait of Richard Willard in the home of Joan and Arthur Fowler of Bratoft, Lincs. Joan is a descendant of the Broad family as Albion (ii)'s sister, Sarah Anne, married George Peter Broad.

Sarah Jane Russell.

Issue:

Sarah Jane, who married Albion Russell (i) at Lewes on January 29 1849. A sampler she stitched in 1882 was until recently in the Hove home of the Russell sisters, daughters of Albion (ii).
Ellen.

The Russell & Bromley Family Tree

MICHAEL (BROMLEY) Clockmaker of Horsham b.1748

WILLIAM THORPE m. MARY FANNIE (first marriage) 1722 Cordwainer b.1747 - d.1819

JOHN (BROMLEY) m. ANN (Gaston) Silversmith of Horsham b.1778 d.1854 — b.1780 - 1840

JOHN CLIFFORD (RUSSELL) m. JANE (Thorpe) 1811 Cordwainer Chichester b.1791 - d.1850 — b.1787 - d.1854

RICHARD WILLARD m. Sarah Cordwainer Lewes b.1780 - d.1843

- MICHAEL (2) b.1812
- ANN b.1809 - d.1855
- JOHN ROGER Alderman b.1814 d.1875
- JANE b.1818 d.1853
- SUSAN b.1816
- JANE b.1847 d.1850
- ANN b.1850 d.1862
- JOHN b.1844 d.1887
- CHARLES
- HENRY HERBERT
- HARRIET b.1812 d.1845
- GEORGE CLIFFORD m. b.1813 d.1874
- CHARLOTTE b.1815 d.1839
- JULIUS m. b.1819 d.1889
- JANE (ANDREWS) b.1824 - d.—
- ALBION RUSSELL m. SARAH JANE (Willard) Shoemaker 1821-1888 — b.1821 - d.1905
- EMILY MARIA (Willard) b.1823 - d.1905
- FANNY CORDELIA b.1859 d.1860
- EDITH b.1861 d.1934
- FREDERICK GEORGE b.1856 d.1858
- GEORGE FREDERICK m. ELIZABETH JANE (RUSSEL) 1874 b.1851 d.1897 — b.1850 d.1893
- ELLEN WILLARD b.1859 d.1859
- GEORGE PETER BROAD m. SARAH ANNIE 1825 Cloth Manufacturer b.1821 d.1901
- ALBION RUSSELL (nick Ally) m. HARRIET (Martha) 1880 Shoemaker b.1858 d.1950 — b.1859 d.1905
- MARGARET EDITH b.1901 d.1988
- HERBERT JOHN m. LIZZIE (Tory) b.1892 d.1918
- ARCHIBALD KATHERINE b.1879
- EDITH GERTRUDE b.1889 d.1950
- BEATRICE MAY b.1889 d.1982
- WILFRED DORIS b.1888 d.1945
- REGINALD m. BUCCLE (Ralph) 1943 b.1894 d.1970
- ARTHUR LESLIE OCTAVIA (Butler-Lind) b.1890 d.1970
- FREDERICK ALBION b.1894 d.1958
- HARRIET b.1895 d.1802
- FLORENCE ALICE b.1891 d.1959
- ERNEST CLIFFORD m. DOROTHY (Whiteman) 1915 Shoe manufacturer b.1893 d.1941
- FREDERICK RUSSELL m. HILDA VIOLET (Underwood) 1918 b.1886 d.1964
- ERNEST WILLARD m. MAUD EDITH (Lucke) b.1827 d.1952 — b.1879 d.1955
- MARGARET WEBSTER m. EDWARD (Carr) b.1916
- PETER b.1920
- ERNEST JOHN "Jack" m. CONNIE (Clegg) b.1911 d.1906
- JUDITH b.1943
- PATRICIA b.1944
- JOHN HILTON b.1949
- FREDERICK KEITH (Toby) m. MARY LOUISE (Drake Williams) 1940 b.1915 d.1959 — m. HELEN (Gessingham) 1960 b.1922 d.1961
- MICHAEL CORNISH m. MARY "MOLLY" (Chybindli) 1959 b.1914
- CHARLES RODERICK KEITH b.1946
- JOHN SEBASTIAN AMBLER WILLIAMS b.1940
- PETER MICHAEL FREDERICK AMERY m. AVRIL ELIZABETH (Kennedy-Kantas) 1966 b.1941
- ROGER JOHN m. KAY (Richard) 1985 b.1943
- NICOLA ANN LYDIA m. ANTHONY JOHNSON 1978 b.1948
- ANDREW MICHAEL JAMES b.1968
- STUART PETER WILLIAM b.1971
- SAMANTHA NICOLA b.1984
- SEBASTIAN MICHAEL b.1986
- VICTORIA SOPHIA b.1989
- EMMA LUI b.1981
- CLAIRE NICOLA b.1985
- ALEXANDER CHARLES b.1987

BIBLIOGRAPHY

Melville's Directory of Hastings.
Reminscences of Horsham. Henry Burstow and William Albery. 1911.
Russell & Bromley Footwear 1820–1996.
Uckfield Fifty Years Ago by David Wood. 1908.
Views and Reviews published by W T Pike, Brighton, *c* 1895.

Newspapers
Sussex Express and County Herald.
Sussex Weekly Advertiser.
West Sussex County Times.